BURN THE BINARY!

Selected Writing on the Politics of Being Trans, Genderqueer and Nonbinary

RIKI WILCHINS

For more information contact:
Riverdale Avenue Books
5676 Riverdale Avenue
Riverdale, NY 10471
www.riverdaleavebooks.com

Design by www.formatting4U.com
Cover by Scott Carpenter
Cover illustration by Blake Chamberlain.

The majority of these articles were published on the Advocate.com between 2007 and 2018 and are used with permission of the author.
Digital ISBN: 978-1-62601-406-0
Print ISBN: 978-1-62601-407-7

First edition, October 2017

Acknowledgments

Special thanks to Camila Saly for taking this volume to heart, and for her incredibly close read. To Clare Howell, for reading everything I ever wrote and then helping select the right pieces—you somehow always make my books come together and make sense. To my publisher, Lori Perkins at Riverdale, for having the idea for this book, and for somehow finding Blake's incredible artwork. To Blake Chamberlain for his creative talent and passion in creating the piece that inspired this book, which then became its cover. And to Gina and Dylan Jade, who tolerate my long late nights writing—you are my life.

Table of Contents

Introduction: An Interview with Riki Wilchins

I met Riki in the fall of 1994 after I'd sought a trans-support group at the Gay and Lesbian Community Center in New York City. Lynn Walker, the moderator of the group I first attended there, steered me to another informal group that met outside the Center. I knew the moment I walked into her apartment that Riki was onto something I needed to know. Each of us got something from that first meeting—she an editor, and me an example of lived experience I could relate to, finally.

This volume is a good sample of Riki's work, beginning with a selection of her articles written for *The Advocate* magazine (Advocate.com, and other outlets), from 2000 through August, 2017, This is followed by selections from *Read My Lips: Sexual Subversion and the End of Gender* (1997), a collection of early writings that highlights her developing theoretical critique of gender and the nature of binaries, illustrated by her experience in confronting life as a young genderqueer. Finally, from *Genderqueer: Voices from Beyond the Sexual Binary* (2002), the anthology she, Joan Nestle, and I edited of works by genderqueers and those who

i

love us, comes a concise explanation of her understanding of the nature of gender and sexuality, and the problems we face.

We begin with an interview I did with Riki, to set the table for what follows:

When I first moved to NYC, I was a rangy Southern lesbian and newly-minted transsexual, trying to figure out how I was going to survive. And then I met you through a mutual friend at a *Menace* meeting, and you were doing this "queer theory" rap and doing some sort of not-exactly-boy-or-girl genderqueer thing, and I thought, "Yeah, that's how I want to do it. If I could."

Except for the fact that I was Midwestern, another rangy lesbian and newly-minted transsexual, and I was still trying to figure out how I was going to do it. But I didn't fit any of the models out there. I didn't really want to wear dresses much or put on make-up. Even when I did, while I sometimes enjoyed it, I didn't look much like a cisgender woman. I had always been a total jock, and I had never had any real sexual attraction to men. So I knew I didn't fit neatly in one of the allowable binary boxes. And I kept talking about genderqueer-ness, about breaking down the categories, and the problems of identity. I knew there was something there (and God knows the old model didn't work for me), but I had no idea what I was talking about. And I kept thinking, "One day, someone is going to tell me what I'm onto." And sure enough, a lesbian feminist friend hooked me up with Judith Butler's *Gender Trouble*, and that kind of ate the next

10 years of my life. It finally gave me a coherent set of tools to understand, and, perhaps more importantly, to finally deconstruct this oppressive gender system I'd been bumping up against since the day I announced my transition. In many ways, queer theory pretty much saved my life, or at least my sanity.

Some people would say that while it was once radical and edgy, postmodernism and what are seen as its offspring, queer and gender theory, is now a spent force. What are your thoughts?

It's probably a bit of a spent force in academia. I'm not sure that it's a spent force in popular culture yet. I'm not sure it will be for some time. Among other things, queer theory offers a very deep and profound critique of how we understand these various Selves— gay, white, trans, etc.—and these bodies we think of ourselves as inhabiting. I think this will take some time to be fully absorbed. At the same time, somewhat like feminism - which some people often describe as an an old or spent force, what that really means is that the things it advocated have moved from the margins to conventional wisdom. For instance, except for the alt-right, everyone now accepts equal pay for equal work, a woman's right to control her own childbearing, that women can be leaders, even presidents, etc. That same kind of intense fertilization of popular culture is now taking place with queerness as well. You can hardly look at any media outlet today and not read someone talking about being "Other": that is a concept straight out of postmodernism. So is the increasing number of kids who refuse to identify as

L, G, B, or T, and just say "I'm genderqueer." We hear increasingly about intersectionality, another concept straight out of Critical Race Theory which is itself connected to postmodernism. And then there's the rise of new, nonbinary identities, which in some ways is the flower of gender theory, one that is just coming into its own. People are finally starting to break down boundaries and identities in very fertile and productive ways. And we're not just militating for the right to change sexes: the whole idea of binary sexes is finally under full assault. So I think we're just starting on a really interesting ride here.

Twenty years ago you were way ahead of the curve on gender, and now it seems that young genderqueers have gone far upstream of that. Many LGBTQ people can only stare in amazement at what they're doing. What are your thoughts on how far, and how quickly, we've come on this issue?

As I wrote in my last book, *TRANS/gressive* (a history of the trans movement), sometimes it seemed it was impossible to make any change at all, and at other times I look back and it feels like it all happened almost overnight. I think things reach a tipping point when they hit critical mass, and things start to take off. I think that's happening here. It took us nearly 20 years to just establish "trans" as an issue. It took about that long for the ideas in queer theory and deconstruction to get intellectual traction, so that people could finally understand that rigid binary gender regimes are both socially constructed and highly oppressive. As a result, now you finally see things taking off politically, socially, and intellectually. But just as trans is finally coming into its own, young people are exploding it and taking it to a whole new place. I tried to point out in Read My Lips that the whole male-to-female / female-to-male transgender paradigm, with which many of us grew up, in many ways required, and even reinforced, a rigid gender binary. So I welcome the fact that some young people are moving beyond this into things like "genderqueer" and "nonbinary." We really do need to burn the binary.

This is your fifth book, coming out right after *TRANS/gressive*, your personal history of transgender activism. Is there an arc to your body of work, and if so where does Burn the Binary! fit in it?

Shortly after my transition, I dedicated a portion of my bookshelves to trans books. There were two: *Gender Outlaw* and *Stone Butch Blues*. I remember liking both, but also realizing in very important ways they were pleas with cisgender culture for understanding, acceptance, even sympathy. You know, mainstream culture feeds on transgender "origin story," where we explain how we've always felt like a little boy or girl (it's always comfortably binary) since we were two or three, or perhaps even back in the womb. I wanted to write the angry trannie book, one that didn't plead for acceptance and wasn't directed at cisgender readers but focused on denouncing oppression and demanding our rights. I wanted to speak directly to other trans and genderqueer people and hopefully give them the tools to articulate the anger they already felt, hopefully in a way that would help radicalize them into realizing that the oppressions they faced were political, they were the fault of a binary gender system, and not that they didn't "pass" well enough, or were born transsexual. And that became *Read My Lips*.

As trans started taking off, you, Joan Nestle and I collaborated on *Genderqueer*, to try to give voice to the full breadth of trans experience coming forward, especially those who no longer fit the neat, cisgender binary discourse of transmen or transwomen. It occurred to me that so many of us could use the ideas of queer theory and postmodernism that I'd found so useful, but they were always couched in impenetrable academic prose. I wanted to put it into high school English, and made it accessible to any genderqueer who needed it. That book became *Queer Theory/Gender Theory*. Then there was a long lull, when I wrote only for myself and didn't publish much. I did keep writing columns for *The Advocate,* and a few other outlets, which I'd been doing on and off since the 1990s, and which makes up the final half of *Burn the Binary!* Around the time of Obama it became clear that transgender was finally going mainstream, and I realized all of the history of our early political activism that really launched transgender rights was in danger of being lost. And that became TRANS/gressive. At first I remember thinking, "Wow, this will be the first book about those of us who launched national transgender political activism." Then by the time I was finished, and had interviewed a lot of the people involved, I was thinking, "Oh, this is going to be the *last* book about those who launched national transgender political activism." Because no one I talked to was planning on writing anything about it. I only hope time proves me wrong.

So in the first book, I was a very angry street activist. There's a lot of humor, but a lot of rage too. By the second book, I'm trying to engage other voices, especially youth who are looking more deeply at queerness and gender. By the third book I'm trying to boil down all the theory into high school English so everyone can access it. By the fourth book I'm looking backwards at over two decades of national transgender political activism. So you could say it tracks in kind of an arc. And then, all the Advocate pieces are me responding to events happening in real time, 800 words at a time.

    —as told to Clare Howell
    August, 2017

Part I
Articles from *The Advocate*, *Advocate.com* and Other Outlets

Creating Child Bodies of Convenience

When X-rays suggested that 12-year-old Karen Waldvogel was going to grow up taller than most other girls, her doctor did what many pediatric endocrinologists do—he overdosed her with estrogen to prevent her growth and, in his mind, increase her chances of one day landing a husband. This is, in effect, Tallness Prevention.

As they doctor had hoped, Karen grew up to stand no taller than 5'11". But, in what she suspects are also results of her early estrogen 'treatment,' Karen also has experienced a truly frightening array of medical complications: excruciating menstruation, hemorrhaging between periods, ovarian cysts, endometriosis, infertility, cervical polyps, and stillborn births. In fact, Karen has since met two other women who underwent similar treatment as adolescents and found that between them they'd had 10 stillborn infants.

What happened to Karen is far from uncommon. According to a February report by the Physicians Committee for Responsible Medicine published in the prestigious *Journal of Pediatric and Adolescent Gynecology*, almost one-third of American pediatric endocrinologists report overdosing their adolescent female patients with estrogen in order to stunt their growth.

And this practice is only one of several socially-sanctioned treatments in which American physicians overdose, cut, or psychologically modify children to make sure they conform to narrow, outdated binary gender norms.

For example, consider intersex infants. About one in every 2,000 births is a child born with atypical genitals. Just as doctors act to prevent 'tallness,' with intersex infants they act to prevent genitals that don't match acceptable male and female. In fact, about 5 infants are cut up each day in American hospitals, simply to make their genitals resemble 'normal' binary male or female. The vast majority of these are otherwise unremarkable infants who have have been diagnosed as having clitorises that are too large.

So why are they cut? Sometimes it's nothing more than the doctor's or the parents' old-fashioned fear that girls with big clits might grow up to be masculine—read: lesbian—women. Boys don't make passes at girls who wear glasses, or, apparently, at girls who have big clits.

Adult survivors of IGM often report lack of sexual sensation, painful urination, extreme feelings of bodily shame, and a host of other physical complications. One child was crippled for life by a series of painful surgeries doctors put him through so he could pee standing up—apparently the *sine qua non* for manhood. Another one was disabled with doctors repeatedly tried to fashion a 6-inch vagina that was far too big for her 5-year-old body to accommodate.

Then, of course, there is Gender Identity Disorder, which most people know as psychiatric diagnosis for transsexuals. But a host of doctors, led by Toronto's Kenneth Zucker, also use the diagnosis in effort to prevent adult homosexuality in so-called 'pre-homosexual' children.

Tallness Prevention, Intersex Genital Mutilation, and Childhood Gender Identity Disorder have two things in common. First, they are all treatments or diagnoses for human conditions that require no medical intervention. And second, they are about ensuring heterosexual gender norms at the expense of alternatives.

There is a multi-million dollar sex industry at work behind the scenes in this country. It's obsessed with bodies, masculinity, genitals, extremes of femininity, and any sign of irregularity. And I'm not talking about prostitutes in short skirts turning tricks on the street. I'm talking about doctors in white coats busily turning babies into "real" men and "real" women.

February, 2005

It's Called Gender Profiling

Even in the best of times genderqueers have faced increased scrutiny or harassment when they travel simply because of the way they look, act, or dress. But as Katie "Zak" Szymanski, a boy-identified dyke, can attest after a recent flight out of New York's JFK, never has this scrutiny been as intense as it has in the months since September 11, 2001.

"First, they made a big deal about whether a male or female officer should pat me down," says Szymanski, who had recently undergone a prophylactic mastectomy due to a family history of breast cancer. "Then they took a lot of time searching my breasts—not because there was anyplace left to hide something there—but because they couldn't figure out why there wasn't more ME there. I was still healing, and it was really painful."

What happened to Szymanski is called "gender profiling." It occurs when a person is singled out solely because they are perceived as not conforming to gender norms. And if you are one of the millions of travelers who happens to be a little butch, a little femme, transgendered, or otherwise "visibly queer," then there's a good chance it may happen to you on your next trip.

Daphne Scholinski, a genderqueer author and trans-identified lesbian, was also targeted when she was trying to catch a flight out of San Francisco, one of the most liberal cities in the country. "Nobody questioned my ID, and my luggage passed right through X-ray," she says. "But they said my belt-buckle was a problem, and made me undo my pants in public—right by the X-ray machine—and pull them down to my thighs."

Added Scholinski, "If I try to defend my rights or talk back, they can label me a trouble-maker. Then I could find myself being strip-searched in custody while my flight takes off. You just have to stand there and take it."

It seemed like just another quiet dinner at the TGIFriday's in Laurel, Maryland when TK—proud nose-guard for the women's professional football team *DC Divas*—got up to use the crowded women's room along with a lot of other women that night. But it wasn't. As she went in, another woman said 'This is the women's room.' TK, unfazed, replied simply, 'I know it is.'

She emerged to find herself confronted by a TGI employee and a uniformed Laurel policeman who was shortly joined by another. TK tried to show identification, which clearly listed her as female. But at no time did anyone ask to see her ID, or even stop to ask what sex she was. Apparently her more masculine gender expression was affront enough so that no one, except of course TK, cared. She shortly found herself face-down on the ground, arm twisted up behind her back, handcuffed and under arrest.

Since she was, in fact, completely female, the only thing they charged TK with was disorderly conduct and disturbing the peace, which in this case translates to her trying really hard to convince the officers that she was indeed female and asking for badge numbers when they refused to listen. She'd been gender profiled.

We're all used to a certain degree of gender inspection. From childhood on, people stare, mock, correct, punish or intimidate us when we cross lines. This is not exactly a new problem, but rather an old problem in a new setting. But when three guys intimidate and harass you and your girlfriend when you're out for a walk, you can at least yell something pithy and then tell the proper authorities about the perpetrators.

In these cases, the perpetrators ARE the proper authorities. There's no one to tell, and pithiness could get you busted. All of which can leave you feeling utterly helpless when confronted with a uniformed genderphobe who's backed up by a National Guardsman with an M-16. You can't change who and what you are just to fly, and you also can't afford to miss the wedding, vacation, or job interview at the end of your flight, so you just shut up and take it.

Reports of gender-profiling have flowed into GenderPAC since September 11, when airlines appropriately increased their focus on security. With that new focus came a dramatic shift in the balance in power, one very much in favor of security personnel— including the phobic few with a strong dislike for anyone who crosses gender lines. What we're seeing is a persistent pattern of travelers being targeted and at times singled out for harsh or invasive treatment because they don't meet someone's ideal of 'real man' or 'real woman.' This kind of prejudice falls disproportionately upon travelers who are gay, lesbian, bisexual, transgender, or queer youth.

One of the reports that especially struck me involved a transsexual who was traveling to the US from Heathrow. Pulled out of line as she was about to board, she was first mocked by a security person who loudly examined her (female) ID, and then she was subjected to a luggage search and full body pat-down as she watched her fellow passengers board.

She made her flight, but complained to airline management, who declined to act. "How many fundamentalist Islamic terrorists do they think travel first class and have sex-reassignment surgery so they can be female?" she asked. "They just didn't like that I was transgender."

The racial profiling of Middle-Eastern fliers is a terrible problem, as recently happened when the FBI detained 26 travelers on four different flights in a single day, because they looked Islamic and had the misfortune of paying cash for one-way tickets. And DWB (Driving While Black) is a similarly a heinous practice that is finally getting some long-overdue attention. But perhaps it's time we also add a new category: "traveling while queer."

The Japanese have a saying: The nail that sticks out gets hammered in. If you're the one that 'sticks out,' the next time you fly or drive, it could happen to you.

January, 2013

On De-transitioning or Mau-mauing the Cisgender Women

Even in these heady times, when it seems every day there's yet another major advance in trans-liberation, simply taking a public leak remains a bitch-and-a-half.

Yes, I know there's an app for that, which will enable your iPhone to locate the nearest gender neutral restroom. And if you you live in downtown Seattle or go to school at UC Berkeley, it probably works great. I usually find the nearest one is at least two time zones away. So I end up trying to choose between liberating the Women's Room, or going back to using the (yuck!) Mens.

Before my transition, I can't say I ever thought much about the Phenomenonolgy of the Men's Room Urinal. But today, I find the idea of a half dozen male strangers standing shoulder-to-shoulder, bleeding their lizards, splashing away in synchronized micturition (thanks, Dude) like it was an Olympic pool event— genuinely terrifying, not to mention a major gross-out. Maybe it's three decades of estrogen kicking in.

I never had to worry about all this because for a long time after I transitioned, I worked hard at presenting as feminine a face as possible. I say 'worked,' because if you're born into a boy-body, then suddenly trying to make it appear reasonably female in your mid-30s is no walk in the park. While I fooled no one, I at least achieved a degree of tolerance from almost everyone.

I could saunter confidently into any restroom that had that outline of a little woman, standing primly in her A-line skirt with her hands at her sides and feet together—you know, the way cisgender women often stand in front of public elevators—and know that if I wasn't her sister, at least all my effort had purchased another Day Pass to FemaleLand. I drew stares, but not blood.

But gradually that effort evaporated. Strip the long hair, earrings, lipstick, mascara and blush of most cisgendered women, and you still usually see a woman. Strip them off me and what you see is... Richard. And no matter how feminine I feel inside, Richard gets no Day Pass. Richard sauntering confidently into the Woman's Room is... chaos.

Some women call out, "It's the Women's Room." The more polite ones run outside to check the sign and make sure it's not *them* who're in the wrong bathroom. Others just glare really hard. I've even had a couple wait outside with their boyfriends to go after me.

And then there are the rare ones who just go off. I was shopping in my favorite high-end South Beach deli one sunny morning when a crazy older woman— not a regular like *moi*—was busy loudly harassing employees. She yelled at the guy behind the meat counter. Then she yelled at the woman working produce.

9

After paying for my exorbitantly expensive goods, I made a beeline for the Women's Room by the registers. Just as I exit my stall, there's Crazy Woman, standing between me and the door. She takes one look, and—although her voice has been in fourth gear all morning—finds that she can still reach that fifth one in overdrive: *"WHAT ARE YOU DOING HERE! THIS IS THE WOMAN'S ROOM! WHAT ARE YOU DOING IN HERE!"*… over and over.

Panicked, I can see employees swarming the room, the manager storming in, the cops being called, and me being forever banned from my beloved deli as I'm perp-walked in shame before the rolling cameras of America's Most Wanted. Because, while I may be legally female back in New York, Florida still goes by chromosomes, and, by those rules, Crazy Woman is the RG (Real Girl).

Somehow without missing a beat I hear myself hollering back at her, "Do I LOOK like a MAN to you?" As this unintentionally zen-like koan stops her in her tracks, I bolt successfully out the door.

Finally, there are those few women I worry I might actually be scaring. No matter how much I want to think of it as "liberating" the Woman's Room by using the bathroom that fits my gender identity (not to mention $25k of surgery), I hate the idea that I might be making another woman afraid.

A trans-activist once told me her Fortune 500 company resolved longstanding disputes about when and whether transitioning MTFs should use the Women's Room with a simple policy known informally as the Bathroom of Least Surprise (BOLS). At the time, such a commonsense formula was a huge step forward for trans-women, over making them jump through the then-common, demeaning hoops of providing doctor's letters, documenting their surgical status, or producing proof of legal sex.

If a transitioning employee would be less surprising using the Women's Room than standing in a dress and high heels at the urinal in the Men's Room, then that's where they should go.

But what happens when you're still playing the role but stop looking the part? As far as transitioning goes, I appear to be a male-to-female-to-male transsexual. My identity has now taken so many turns they could make it into a ride at DisneyWorld.

So I wonder—even though I am now definitely more surprising in the Women's Room, can I still demand that the world recognize and honor my inner femme? Can I refuse to to do an intelligible gender while still demanding the privileges that fit with womanhood?

I've heard similar concerns about the Woman's Room from mega-butch lesbian friends, who get hassled just like I do but seem to be able to muster a sense of entitlement to the space that remains out of my reach.

I turned to the Brown Boi Project for advice from masculine-identified women. In their kicky video *It Gets Messy In Here,* one recounts how, out of patience, she turned on one harasser and shouted, "I have a V-A-G-I-N-A-!!!" Now there's an interesting technique. I can do that. In fact, it's something I can practice at home in front of my mirror.

Les Feinberg used to say that stone butches going quietly about their business in the Women's Room

11

aren't really hassled because other women genuinely feel afraid; they're hassled because other women are pissed off at their appearance.

This should make me feel better. But I've also found that door swings both ways. I was finishing up my business in the Womens' Room at the NYC Gay Community Center where I'd been organizing transgender support groups, when in walks this guy. I'm not exactly happy, but I hold my tongue.

Now, the Community Center is a genuinely safe and welcoming space, and one of the few where I could access the Women's Room without worrying about how I happened to look—a huge relief.

This makes it a precious resource. Even more so in a gay-male-dominated building (they had the huge Mens Room with the giant Keith Haring sex mural that is now worth more than the entire building that houses it; we had a small room with no mural, by Keith or anyone else).

So I wasn't feeling threatened, just kind of offended that even in this one, small (dare I say it?) women-only space... well, you get the idea. But then this guy starts getting undressed. And as he pulls off his pants right in front of me, I turn and ask him, 'Really? Really??'

And as he starts yelling at me something I can't quite catch, he pulls a green dress from his bag and I realize this is someone—pre-transition, post-transition, non-transition?—who came to the Center for one of my support groups and, like me, considered the Women's Room safe harbor.

A few seconds of privilege had turned me from a right-on, in-your-face, transgender activist into a radical lesbian feminist intent keeping the men and trannies out of the Michigan Womyn's Music Festival. Which is to say, the door of gender tolerance swings both ways, Buster, and it had just swung back and hit me in the ass.

To this day I never question anyone I see in the restroom based on their appearance. I'd just like to be afforded the same privilege. But that's a long, long story. Before we get started, does anyone need to go?

January, 2014

"Where Have All the Butches Gone?"

When I was doing more public speaking, I used to do a little experiment. I'd be asked to address gay groups on the problem of gender. As they all looked at me expectantly, I would invite them to discuss *their* problem with gender. This inevitably drew a lot of blank looks, especially with all-male groups. So I would ask them, 'How many of you are gay?'

They would all proudly raise their hands. Then I'd ask, 'How many of you are bottoms?' Everyone's hand went down, fast, really fast. Then they'd all look at the one, self-identified fairy who still had his hand up and laugh. Apparently gay male communities are composed entirely of tops and tough guys. No wonder dating is so difficult!

And then I'd ask them what was so humiliating, here in the 21st century, to admit that just once—when you were young, drunk, didn't know what you were doing—just that once you were... a catcher instead of a pitcher?

And it was the gender thing. Being a bottom meant taking the "women's role" in bed. No one wanted to admit to that publicly. No one wanted to be recognized as *being* any way visibly womanly, of *being* gender nonconforming. That was stretching gay pride too far.

Where have all the butches gone?

This question was first posed to me by Joan Nestle, who was personally responsible for resuscitating butch/femme in the 1980s after it had fallen into the dust-bin of political correctness (yes, it did seen like nearly all lesbians, urban and country, dressed in plaid shirts and boots for a while there).

As a bone-deep femme herself, she was not referring to an absence of butch-identified women, but the sudden disappearance, as in a mass, silent, migration, of vast numbers of them from the lesbian community.

In a sense, she was a victim of both her own success and the advances of medical science. While she made it safer for tens of thousands to embrace their inner butch, the emergence of transgender activism and the new proliferation of Vitamin T (testosterone) made it possible for a significant minority to embrace their inner FTM as well.

In the 1970s, it seemed like to be transsexual was to be a "male-to-female" transwoman. Even the doctors reported that they saw three or four transwomen for every transman. Being transgender, it seemed, was largely (if not exclusively) something for those of us who were XY.

But that turned out to be largely an artifact of surgery and history. The first trannies who were outed as such were (the prehistoric) Lily Elbe, (the early, early) Christine Jorgenson, and (the later-but-still early) Jan Morris. This was simply, and unfortunately, because it was much more practical to do MTF 'bottom surgery' than FTM. *Easier to make a hole than a pole*—surgeon's humor.

As the boundaries of transgender began to shift with new visibility and activism, and it became more acceptable to live as your correct sex with or without a complete surgical makeover, suddenly the numbers of FTMs skyrocketed. The guys started showing up at the same doctors and clinics as the gals. And among them were many who had lived for years as butches. The effect was the disappearance of many butches from the lesbian community that Joan bemoaned.

Where have all the butches gone?

This was the same question I asked myself throughout the rise of trans-activism. When transgender people were attacked, where were the butches and femmes? As the part of the gay community most identified with gender and affected by gender intolerance, why were they never there showing solidarity? Why were they never organized? Why was there never a specifically butch/femme voice seeking political representation, visibility, and recognition? There were certainly butch/femme organizations, but all the ones I knew of were social or historical in nature.

For that matter, where were all the effeminate gay men? There were the Radical Faeries (not to mention the cheeky Sisters of Perpetual Indulgence), but, again, they were mostly personal and social, lacking any political edge or political agenda.

This was an important question, because in past decades the visible face of the gay community were the butches, fairies, and drag queens. They were the ones your mom and mine "just knew" were gay. They were the ones who were "visibly queer," who embarrassed more closeted gays and made straight people uncomfortable. They were what "obvious homosexuals" looked like before we all were promoted to good, normal gays.

More to the point, they were the ones who couldn't or wouldn't pass as heterosexual and too many of them had scars—both psychological and physical—to show for it.

For many years, the now-defunct GenderPAC fought long and hard to keep our political activism 'gender rights' instead of 'transgender rights,' so the movement was open and accessible to those non-transgender gays who were genderqueer—for people, in other words, who never showed up.

Where have all the butches gone?

This was also the question I asked myself as I sat among 200 folks, drawn from the very top of the pyramid of gay political leaders, at one of the country's largest liberal foundations last month. Sitting around me was everybody who was anybody, ready for broad-ranging discussions of the past, present, and future of the modern LGBTQ movement.

We talked about all the identities in the rainbow—gay men, bisexuals, transgender kids, lesbians. Everyone, that is, except for butches and fairies. In some ways, it was a fascinating display of communal myopia. It was as if all adult gayness was gender normative, except for transgender people and a few gender-fluid kids.

Our politics still resembles our personal ads: "No

butches" for women, and "straight looking and acting only" for men. Gender-phobia is still at the heart of modern gay consciousness and gay pride. There may be private acceptance of gender difference, but when it comes to political visibility, for all intents and purposes, we may as well be straight.

I no longer expect gay leaders to discuss butchness or effeminacy, but I find it sad and amazing that even the butches and fairies *in the room* never mention gender oppression as an important facet of gay politics—theirs or anyone else's.

Where have all the butches gone?

Until we are less embarrassed to be genderqueer, we will not find them. They will remain invisible, hidden in plain sight, even though they are all around and in front us. In fact, those strong silent butches are there, right over there... right next to all those sweet, effeminate fairies. But we won't notice them, and they won't ask for our political notice either.

We Happy Trans: Undoing Gender

It was *Gender Trouble* (1990), and other writings by Judith Butler, that first ignited my thinking about gender, and made me believe a transgender politics that transcended both the binary and the demands of cisgendered people was possible. There was a period of about three years when I seemed helpless to do anything but discuss and analyze gender theory, even over the most casual luncheon dates. Being able to finally deconstruct the oppression with which I struggled, and see all the moving parts, ignited in me a new desire to confront rather than conform to the gender system, and informed my trans-activism for the coming two decades.

So I looked forward to eagerly devouring her ideas on contesting gender oppression when her book, *Undoing Gender* (2004) was published. But her ideas of what passed for gender activism seemed strangely oblique and bloodless to me—small, individual acts of insubordinacy that parodied and upset gender norms, while celebrating genderqueerness. WTF?

In Margaret Nussbaum's well-publicized attack

on Butler's cosmology ("The Professor of Parody," *The New Republic.* 22:37-45, 1999) she pinpointed the absence of such messy realities as organizing, policy change, and legislation—things to which I was now devoting my life. What was the point of being a happy gender warrior doing private acts of rebellion? How on earth was this going to be the big stick that would overturn an ubiquitous binary gender system?

The idea of embracing parody or celebration is in itself foreign to me. One of the primary attacks of radical feminists on trans-women like me was that were parodying "real women," by appropriating their body parts, clothing and gestures. At the same time, non-radical guys on the street attacked me for simply not being *real*, period. Parody seemed to be the very air I was forced to breathe—hardly a great foundation on which to build personal or political liberation.

And whither celebration? What was there to celebrate about being male? I had spent a lot of time and money—not to mention losing my job, family and life partner—in order to live a womanhood that almost everyone not in my immediate circle of family and friends (and, privately, many of those as well) seemed intent upon denying me.

And it wasn't just nasty straight people, either: Women's groups rejected transwomen; lesbian groups ejected us; Gay pride parades didn't include transgender; State and national "LGB" organizations simply refused to 'add the T.'

And then there was the isolation. In the 1970s, there was only one other transsexual in Cleveland that anyone knew of at the time, Carmen. She pretty much held me together through my surgery and basically kept me from killing myself as I watched my social support system quietly dissolve. When I heard from her about Joan, we were three. Our numbers had grown by 50% in a city of almost a million.

And the shame. It somehow felt deeply shameful to keep telling folks I was something they didn't agree that I was, that I didn't particularly appear to them to be, and that almost no one recognized or honored. I'd get on a subway car and watch young boys start staring, trying to read me, and then pointing and finally laughing and taunting.

My solution was to begin wearing a black *Transexual Menace* T-shirt that no one could miss. My motto was 'don't read me—read my shirt.' I wore one every single day for three years, even when I flew in to organize demonstrations in states like Texas, Nebraska, or Georgia where I felt my safety was at issue.

It was around that time that Holly Boswell, a transgender spiritual leader, used to tell people, "Congratulations, you're transgendered." I had no idea what she was talking about.

Fast forward 20 years, and we have the rise of a whole generation of transgender kids who understand their bodies as a place of pride, identity, power and yes… celebration.

How else to explain Warren Beatty and Annette Benning's FTM son, Stephen Ira Beatty, who created a video outing himself on the *WeHappyTrans* website which went viral and was viewed over a million times. Or Sadie, the 11-year-old girl who wrote an open letter to President Obama complimenting his mentioning gays and lesbians in his Inauguration speech, but reminding him to mention transgender children like her.

Sadie went on to write of the fear and ostracism transgender kids often face, even as she affirmed to him her deep pride and joy in being transgender. The letter was posted online by her parents, quickly picked up by the *Huffington Post*, and then was reposted widely.

Or even Gregory Gorgeous, whose YouTube celebration of his profound and beautiful genderqueerness has become an underground phenomenon, generating nearly 50 million page views.

It may not be the duty, but it is certainly the fate of activists to often create political advances of which they, themselves, are unable to fully partake. I recall the wonderful Larry Kramer standing up at a meeting to remind anyone who was tempted to slack off, that, "They hate us! They hate us out there!" He'd been right once, but this room was filled with multi-millionaire and billionaire gay donors, and this was just as *Will & Grace* was becoming a middle America hit.

So, when I was invited to cut a video for *It Gets Better*, I agreed, because it really does get better. But I could no more cut a video for *WeHappyTrans* than I could levitate while filming it. My public "coming out" gesture was not an online celebratory post, but donning a Menace T-shirt in order to survive in a time and place when being trans didn't mean being young and fabulous, but isolated, invisible, and taunted. For me, the emerging transgender activism exists in a land that I don't inhabit, and even that I cannot yet visit.

Yet, even as I remain deeply committed to traditional political organizing, I realize that every time a parent stands behind their openly transgender daughter, every time an out transgender child writes an open letter to the President, every time a celebrity transgender son comes out, all these small, isolated, individual acts of personal insubordinacy together are challenging the binary, overturning gender oppression, and, yes, even undoing gender.

April, 2013

F*cking Cis-People

One of the pleasures (and occasional pains) of writing a column online is reading the comments complete strangers leave. It wasn't even in response to something I'd written, but rather to another commenter, that Rufus Rufushy Ulrik wrote the two-word imprecation I can't get out of my mind: "fucking cis-people."

Only that, nothing more. To my ear, it's even more effective than Danah Gaz's "Die Cis-scum," which has an over-the-top edge of goth hostility to it, a take-off on a Ross Meyer 1950's trash flick, *Faster Cis-Pussycat! Kill! Kill!*

But "fucking cis-people" resonates for me in ways I'm still coming to grips with, right down to its note of plaintive resignation. No exclamation point, no caps. More of a sigh than an expletive. It crystallizes something I've been feeling for a long time, but couldn't put into words.

You see, I have struggled with my fair share of those twin demons of all despised minorities who have the misfortune to be nomadic, wandering in search of a cultural heritage and a geography of acceptance: shame and self-loathing.

There is, after all, no transgender section of any city. Even in New York City, where I can find people like me, unlike so many other minorities—Lubovitchers, African-Americans, gays, Italians—there is no place we can call our own, where *we* are the norm, where we see ourselves constantly reflected in eyes of others. So I wander through other people's lands as Other. Even my presence within the LGB and sometimes T community is remains highly contested.

And before my status as "trannie," there was transition. Practically the first thing my doctors did was make sure I really wanted to be a cisgendered woman, because what other kind of woman could I want to be? I couldn't very well tell them I wanted to be a transgender woman or a genderqueer. Being a 'true transsexual' was *defined* by the very act of wanting not to be one.

When I was prompted to explain that I felt "like a woman, trapped in man's body" (thanks, but no, I'm just trapped in the wrong culture), I was explaining that my deepest identification—the one that had driven me to give up family and lover and jobs and, yes, body parts—was with those whom I was not: cisgendered people.

Having established that I wanted to be a cisgendered woman, my doctors then rushed to assure me that I could not be one. For instance, I would have something called a "blind vagina" (which curiously did not move me to inquire if my new vagina would need a seeing-eye pussy).

I was to have other "shortcomings" cisgenderwise: I wouldn't lactate, drop eggs, menstruate, get pregnant. They enumerated a veritable cis-copia of things I was supposed to desperately want yet could not have.

To be fair, I think they did this not to drive me from depression to suicidal depression, a journey for which I had already packed my bags and hardly needed their assistance. They acted to insulate themselves from my claims of malpractice when I was inevitably disappointed with hormonal and surgical outcomes that failed to liberate the inner, true cis-me.

And then, of course, there was, as always, passing.

Passing—as a cisgendered female, what else?—was *the* grand finale. To be truly successful I should look just like what I was not, a cisgender woman. Moreover, real success meant the audience (and trans-people never lack for an audience, no?) observing my little gender performance would never realize that I was succeeding. If they became aware that I was succeeding, then I had failed.

So I entered my transition with both an overwhelming desire to succeed—a yearning to be what I was not and could never be—and a growing suspicion, laced with not a little resentment, that the cosmology I had bought into had embedded me in a conundrum from which there was no escape, and no possibility of redemptive self-esteem.

We end up in this contested space where we're supposed to look up to and want to be cis-people, while at the same time we're supposed to accept all the terrible things they think about us. Our bodies become the ground for cis-people to work out their craziness and discomfort and fear around gender.

They get to use their standards and appearance to define the bodies and identities to which we are allowed to aspire, and then judge us on how well we do at approximating them. And, oh yeah, I forgot to add, we're also dependent on them for things like housing, jobs, and (often) partners. If they don't like us, we don't get a lease, or they don't hire us, or they fire us, or we never get a date. Lovely system.

Which gets me back to "fucking cis-people." I don't hold it against cisgendered people that I swallowed all this crap for a long time—hook, line, and sinker. Or that it's taken me so long to purge my system of it, as if it were a particularly diffuse, slow acting poison. After all, they were playing the game the way they were taught it, just as I was.

What I do hold against them, and continue to find appalling, is that all the insulting and soul-decaying things I believed about myself came from them, and had cis-fingerprints all over them.

There are very nasty notions in the cultural ether about transgender people, and, my friends, they do not originate with us. To put it bluntly: there is nothing positive in the cisgendered world about transpeople. NOT. ONE. THING. It's as if the cosmology of cisgender society is toxic to transpeople—our kryptonite.

Nor is it only the wing-nuts who think this way. How about that hipster, post-ironic, post-modern icon, *South Park*? South Park has an endearing way of puncturing the great and mighty, so it can stick up for the weak and oppressed, like gay people.

Except when it comes to us. Liberal America laughed right along as they compared sex change surgery to being surgically altered to be a fish. That's how ridiculous we are—changing a man into a woman? Might as well try to turn him into a fish! What could be funnier than watching a man waddle around on flippers because he felt like a fish trapped in a man's body. Just think of all the transgender kids out there, getting the shit kicked out of them in school each day, who get to tune in at night and see this. Gosh, are we trannies funny, or what? And here I mean not only "funny ha-ha," but also "funny peculiar."

And what about the transphobic reader comments that will inevitably materialize below this piece, if the past is any guide? Like the commenter who kept referring to me as "That bitch," as in, "That bitch ought to have her children taken away from her."

Or Bethany, who asked, "Which part of Riki is female exactly? The inside out penis?" (Original riposte, Bethany!) Or Nick, who observed that I'm "delusional and can't accept Biological reality." Or Anthony, who recommends that we all just "drop TB form LGBT and get back to the original" (Right on, bro.) Or Cathy, who calls me "this prick," and pines for a real lesbian who can counter my "woman-hating bullshit" (by this she means a cisgendered woman, of course).

These are just a small sample from the posts that weren't removed for being aggressively hostile, profane, or transphobic, and we're talking about *The Advocate*, the leading online magazine for the progressive LGBT community. I was thinking I might be preaching to the choir here, but a lot of it turns out to be the Moral Majority in drag.

Being part of cis-society is very complicated, not to say borderline abusive. They don't really get us. Even many of our friends. Perhaps, when your mind is so strictly bordered by Male and Female with nothing in between, you simply can't understand. You just don't have a space in your head for "transgender *and* woman" or "transgender *and* man," or simply for "genderqueer."

Sometimes it's like having a mother you really wish would like you, but who instead constantly withholds acceptance, and tells you you're not enough, and keeps pointing out your perceived shortcomings. Which is to say, sometimes it really, really sucks.

Well, I didn't like my mom all that much either, bless her heart. She didn't get me. Sometimes it's just time to leave home. Alas, we all have a life sentence here in Cis-World.

F*cking cis-world.

September, 2013

Attack of the 6-Foot Intersex People

I first met Cheryl Chase 15 years ago. She was, to say the least, striking: intense, charismatic, brilliant, and, oh yeah… really, really angry.

Cheryl had been born Charlie, until doctors decided he was really she, and his small penis was her overly large clitoris. So they operated, and cut it down to better resemble a "normal" girls'. They told Cheryl's mom that she must never acknowledge any of this to her daughter, that she must, in fact, lie to her own daughter if she was ever asked about it. Because, they thought, a child knowing that his or her genital sex was in any way ambiguous would be so traumatic as to be devastating. This was standard clinical practice at the time, and sadly, in too many places, it still is.

As she grew, Cheryl realized something was wrong. For one thing, she had little genital sensation, and couldn't experience sexual pleasure in that area. And then there were also the obvious signs that someone had operated on her body.

It took her years of searching to find out the truth of what had been done to her, and why she felt so wrong

30

and so different. She grew up deeply depressed. By the time she was a world-class technology programmer and living part-time in Japan—she speaks fluent Japanese—she was completely suicidal, and only avoided taking her own life because she feared it would bring shame and cultural ostracism upon her hosts.

Part of what was slowly killing her was the sheer isolation and loneliness of being the only one in the world. So Cheryl did what every accidental activist has done for centuries—she organized.

She founded the Intersex Society of North America (ISNA), the world's first intersex advocacy organization. She told me at the time that she did it mostly to find other people, to see if there was anyone else out there like her.

And this is a fine juncture for a sidebar on language. Although in the past Cheryl has tolerantly allowed me to refer to her as *The Head Herm*, intersex people don't ever use the term *hermaphrodite* (if they ever did), which in any case was never accurate, and actually derives from the Greek figure of Hermaphroditus, who had a female body with male genitals.

Most of us think of intersex as 'people born with both sets of genitals'—a condition so rare as to practically qualify as an urban myth.

Intersex—the new term is Disorders of the Sex Development (DSD)—covers a cluster of conditions of chromosomal or anatomic sex at birth, most of which are non-threatening and have little or no clinical or medical significance. Cheryl used to talk about them as 'unexpected genitals,' but I think the really crucial thing about them is that these are genitals that make doctors uncomfortable. So they have to do something about it.

Naturally this means doing something to change the infant, not their own discomfort.

Current clinical standards still call for cutting up intersex kids, the earlier the better, so they have genitals that better resemble yours and mine.

Well, *yours* anyway.

Cheryl pithily defined DSD as a psychological emergency on the part of doctors, treated by performing surgery on the body of the infant. That sums it up. It's done as compassionate surgery, and often performed for free. But that does nothing to ease its sheer awfulness and barbarity, or the terrible waste of lives and young bodies.

Cheryl and I eventually started a protest group—yes, an intersex protest group—irreverently named after ISNA's occasional newsletter: *Hermaphrodites With Attitude!* With Transexual Menace folks, we'd show up outside big name pediatric conventions and major urban hospitals—practically all of them do intersex surgery—and picket.

The doctors and medical staff simply didn't know what to make of us; they looked on as if they were under attack! Real life hermaphrodites! In matching T-shirts! With nasty picket signs!

Well, we knew then that the surgery—intrusive, unnecessary, irreversible and utterly lacking in the most basic notions of informed patient consent—was ripe for medical malpractice suits. Cheryl and I would sometimes daydream about how things might be different for future DSD kids if only there was a way to file lawsuits.

But the statute of limitations always had run out by the time children grew into (angry, aware) adults.

And parents never sued. And even if they wanted to, there was no national organization with lawyers and funding and expertise to back them up.

Now. There. Is.

With help from *Advocates for Informed Choice*, a South Carolina couple has filed a landmark lawsuit against state doctors and social workers for unnecessary genital surgery on their 16 month-old child. The *Southern Poverty Law Center* joined AIC in the suit.

Pamela Crawford, the mother, declared, "We feel very strongly that these decisions to permanently alter somebody's genitalia and their reproductive ability for no medical reason whatsoever is an abhorrent practice and can't be continued. It is too late for our son, the damage has been done to him."

The child, identified to only as M.C., had been in the foster system when doctors noted the genital ambiguity and decided they would remake the genitalia—and the child—as female. Alas, M.C., who is now 8, identifies as male and has been living as a boy. God only knows what awaits him as an adult with the body these doctors decided it was their right to create.

M.C. is only one of multitudes. Dozens of these surgeries take place every day in US hospitals. If this took place abroad, we'd call it by it's real name: genital mutilation. A US District Court Judge has already ruled that this unnecessary surgery on DSD kids could violate the Constitution, denying a State motion for dismissal.

The doctors and the State are refusing comment, claiming its pending litigation. No doubt they feel...under attack! By real-live hermaphrodites! With lawyers! Filing nasty lawsuits!

Well, here's hoping they see many more nasty lawsuits. This dark, medieval corner of negligent malpractice needs to be pulled kicking and screaming into the light of day. Federal lawsuits have a way of doing that. They also will go a long way towards making doctors and hospitals, who believe it is their right to carve gender stereotypes into the bodies of uncomplaining infants, think twice, before they operate.

The landmark actions of the Crawfords and AIC have brought that time one day closer. Here's hoping other parents follow. This practice must stop.

September, 2013

Man, *Definitely* Don't Try Me

Another hot 4th of July. Here in Washington, DC, the gay community is cheering the enormous victories for gays rights, especially marriage equality and the Supreme Court decision. So much progress.

And yet over an eight-day period, two transgender women were shot and wounded, two more stabbed, and another violently assaulted. One stabbing victim was cut or stabbed 40 times before managing to run for help and collapsing in the street.

The assault is especially worrisome for me, since it took place at a 24-hour pizza take-out on my corner. When I go by on my 5:00 morning runs, I always considered it a safe oasis in the dark, if someone tried to mug me. Maybe not.

A drag performer who stopped in at 3:00 a.m. from a nearby bar was assaulted by two women who called him a "tranny" and "faggot" as they slapped, beat, and punched him and pulled out his hair. Employees stood around watching, not bothering to intervene or call the police. A half dozen young male bystanders cheered. One put up a video of the incident on YouTube for its entertainment value. What could be more fun than watching a diminutive drag queen get *tuned up* by two violent women?

It was reminiscent of the brutal beating last year of Chrissy Lee Pollis by two enraged women at a suburban Maryland McDonald's not far from here, filmed by an employee who also declined to intervene, as Pollis was pummeled into having a seizure. And we're not halfway through the summer.

DC is and remains the epicenter of transgender violence in the US. When we asked young men in Southeast DC, where many of the attacks take place, why the rate is so high, they replied that the most feared prisoners in the federal penitentiary systems are the ones from DC and South Philly. More than Compton, more than the South Bronx. Because they are so violent and so quick to resort to violence.

But I wonder if that's all of it. There are also stories of transgender sex workers taking Amtrak down on weekends from as far away as New York City so they can work the DC streets because the trade is so good. It may be that DC has a special, if unspoken, custom of males hooking up with transgender women.

I recall most vividly the dual murders of Ukea Davis and Stephanie Thomas here in DC in 2003. I remember it so well because even among crimes of surpassing brutality, it stood out. The two teenagers went out for some smokes late one night, and while sitting in their car, a driveby shooter sprayed them both with automatic weapons fire. It gets worse. The shooter parked his car, walked back to the two dead girls, and then shot both their bodies again as they lay dead in their car.

For all these years, I've tried to comprehend that level of hatred, of violent transphobia—to park and deliberately walk back like that to shoot them some more.

Yet when we focus-grouped young men in Southeast DC, where many of the attacks take place, they told us this might not have been an especially transphobic attack, perhaps not even a hate crime in the traditional sense. Their conviction was that the guy had probably had intimate relations with one or both of them, and this was his way to cover his tracks and maintain his street cred.

Eventually these young men, recruited by one of DC's model community-based programs, Community Education Group, helped us identify six attitudes driving the violence against transgender women:

1. I don't get transgender woman, and they make me uncomfortable.
2. Transgender women are an offense to my manhood and masculinity.
3. Transgender women are always coming on and trying to test me.
4. Transgender women are frauds who are trying to deceive me.
5. If my friends see I know a transgender woman or she knows me, soon they will start taunting and avoiding me. I have to attack her to show them I'm still a man.
6. I've been attracted to or had intimate relations with a transgender woman, and the only way to restore my manhood is to violently attack and reject her.

In some ways, the last two are the most interesting and confounding. It's the children's game of infection/inoculation played on elementary school playgrounds the world over: if a girl touches me or I like a girl or she likes me, I'm infected with her "cooties," and all the other boys will tease and avoid me. I must take some kind of aggressive action (pushing her to the ground, shoving her, throwing a ball at her) to innoculate myself and restore my manhood and social status.

Unfortunately, this game is being played by adults, and for keeps. As one man told us, if a transgender woman even showed she knew him in passing on the street, his friends would start teasing him and asking why and how well he knew her. In a week, they'd stop riding in the same car with him. And, within a month, they'd start wondering if he was a "fag" too, and stop speaking to him. Restorative violence is, ,then, his only way to combat the taint of a possible homosexual encounter or attraction and recover his street masculinity.

I've been working with longtime DC activists like Earline Budd and Dana Beyer, with help from the Mayor's Office of LGBTQ Affairs, to think through what kind of anti-violence program might help stop the cycle of assaults.

What do you do with a masculinity that is still so fragile that simply being acknowledged by a transgender woman constitutes a social taint worthy of violence, and intimate contact—which would result in social death—is grounds for deadly assault?

Perhaps it's best to close with the voices of the young men themselves, and what we learned from them.

1. There is no distinction between transgender women and gay men: A fag is a fag.

   "What is the difference between gay and transgender? You just made the word longer."

   "It ain't like they're apples and oranges; they're all apples."

2. Manhood is drilled into Black men from birth; they fight every day to maintain it—it is infuriating that gay men and transgender women reject masculinity.

   "Your father, your mother, your uncle, your aunt, your cousins, your sisters, your brothers have been installing in your mind that this is the shape of a man, this is what a man is, this is what a man does. So you shouldn't be doing that. If I'm one of these young pitbulls on the street, if I see something that look to me like— who is this n*gger looking like my mama?"

3. Gay men and transgenders are always flirting and testing your manhood and you have to respond violently.

   "This mother f*cker drag queen looked at me. I'm thinking, Oh, is this mother f*cker trying me? Automatically, you're like, let me straighten this out and establish that, 'Hey, I'm a man. I don't f*ck around.'"

   "That's cool, as long as you just keep that sh*t over there. Don't try to push that off on me. And don't be trying me on the street either. Definitely don't try me."

39

4. "Passing" by transgender women is a fraud that seeks to deceive men into being falsely attracted to them.

"It's more the deception piece. The issue isn't what they're doing, what they look like. It's when they try to put what they do on you."

In Chinatown last year, Ahmad Robinson allegedly asked a transgender woman, "Are you a bitch or n*gga?" When she replied, "What the fuck does it look like?" Robinson then allegedly said, "Motherfucka, you got a dick," and then assaulted her.

I treasure the acceptance gays, lesbians and bisexuals are getting now. Their victories are hard won, and deserved. Lesbian and gay rights seem to go from strength to strength today, generating headlines and creating the sense that the LGBT community has finally arrived.

Yet in the midst of this success, transgender women remain an endangered class, the targets of deeply held attitudes and hatreds we are just beginning to understand. I can find no national organization or gay funder that prioritizes stopping transgender violence. As our organizations and philanthropic institutions devote more of their resources to things like gay marriage here in DC and elsewhere, our community's most vulnerable members—young, low-income, female, and of color—continue dying. I wonder, will we hear them?

And a Child Shall Lead Them

It was almost 20 years ago—in 1994 or 1995—that I found myself yelling at the head of the Human Rights Campaign and one of its top legal advisors about their workplace rights bill, the Employment Non-Discrimination Act (ENDA). The former is now my sister-in-law, the latter head of the EEOC.

This highlights the very first law of Washington: it's a very small town, so be careful with whom you pick fights. It *will* come to bite you in the ass. The discussion kept pivoting around the assertion that sexual orientation needed federal legislation, but gender identity could be handled through the courts.

Naturally we pressed loud and hard for a single, unified bill, rather than an endless series of legal struggles that no one in the room was prepared to pay for and which would, in any case, face final adjudication by the always-hostile "Supremes" (of the Supreme Court).

This was before the LGB movement had morphed into the LGBT movement for good. Transpeople were still widely considered not only disposable but an impediment to bills like ENDA, and later, in the states, bills like NY's SONDA, New York's version of ENDA.

Which was better, went the question of the moment, passing a good bill that would protect 98% of the community now, or waiting 10, 20, or 30 years—who knew how many?—to pass the perfect bill that would protect 100%?

Nor was this a minority opinion. Congressman Barney Frank, the reigning head of gay politics in the United States House of Representatives, had opined that being trans-inclusive was a deal-killer. That was that. As one Democratic Congressional office told us, "No one is going to get to the left of Barney on gay rights."

Congressman Frank was worried that transpeople and cisgender folks showering in the same bathrooms were a combustible combination that would make ENDA go up in flames. Although, I should add that I have never met a pre-op trannie with an unquenchable hunger to find cisgender people to take showers with. Or maybe it was just the fear of this specter that he was worried about.

Indeed, after we organized the first National Gender Lobby Day, the Family Research Council (FRC) put out a nasty little cartoon summarizing our efforts around ENDA with Private Maxwell Klinger of M*A*S*H in a dress, demanding his right to work in the office as a woman. And that was their A-game, folks.

No matter. Gender identity and trans-people were excised from the version of ENDA that finally passed the (Democratic) House, but predictably died in the (Republican) Senate.

Of course today things are completely different. ENDA finally passed the (Democratic) Senate, but then died a slow death in the (Republican) House. *Plus ça change...*

It appears that we finally have an answer to the

question posed in that first meeting: "How many years would it set back ENDA to enable pre-op trannies to indulge their pathological need to shower naked around cisgender folks?" In fact, for all the anger and angst we've expended on it, the issue of transpeople and ENDA, like Elvis, has quietly left the building.

In a sign of how much the dialog has shifted, even Rep Dan Coats (R-IN), a dedicated wingnut if ever there was one, and the only Senator to speak out against ENDA (read that again slowly: *the only Senator to speak out against ENDA...),* devoted his entire 12 minute speech to just about everything *but* transgender people, showered or dry. His main issues seemed to be with jurisprudential over-reach and the protection of religious-minded employers.

Alas FRC, like Old Faithful, has not changed its playbook quite as much. We're still in there, but trans-intrusion into bathrooms are the *seventh* item down in a 13-item shopping list of misinformed objections ('...would allow some biological males, who claim to be female, to appear nude before females (and vice versa) in bathrooms, locker rooms, and showers.')

Where is Mad Max Klinger when we need him?

Transpeople are in real danger of moving all the way from social freaks to acceptable shower-mates. Talk about your gender spectrum! I suspect that part of this shift is due to transgender kids. When I was running GenderPAC, we'd get calls every few months from some publicity-hungry media outlet in the midst of a rating sweep—it was always television—asking for help locating a transgender person they could interview and get good, titillating before-and-after pictures of transitioning, since cisgender viewers love this shit.

The teaser practically writes itself and hasn't budged an inch since Christine Jorgenson found her Danish doctor: *Ex-GI Becomes Blonde Beauty!!!*

We always refused to help, considering this kind of salacious coverage exploitative rather than informative. They usually found some cooperative trannie eager for the publicity anyway.

But then they changed tactics entirely, and (unintentionally) finally did some good. What really helped shift the dialog on trans, what really helped spike the right-wing cannons, was not just decades of transgender activism and people like me yelling at people like you.

No, what has helped turn the tide has been a cascade of stories like, *"Transgender at 6: For Tyler and His Parents, No Second Thoughts,"* and *"Colorado Transgender Girl, 6, Wins Discrimination Case,"* and *"Transgender Girl Crowned Homecoming Queen at California School,"* and *"Iowa Crowns Transgender Homecoming Queen."* (Iowa? Really?)

Now you can argue that adult trannies like me are indecent perverts. But what do you do with a six-year-old who just wants to wear a dress and play dolls with her friends? It's clearly not his/her "lifestyle," or "personal choice," or any of those other tricky right-wing euphemisms designed to obscure the fact that gender identity is hard-wired from birth, and there's nothing we can do about it.

No, right now, transgender children are leading the fight and winning. Simply being who they are refutes nearly every argument our foes want to make. It's truly a case of "and a child shall lead them."

Six-year-olds Tyler and Cory are both in

elementary school, and I sincerely doubt that either of them dreams of one day growing up to shower naked with their cisgender classmates. What they do dream of, or at least probably will, when they get a little older, is being accepted, being left in peace, and having the same choices and opportunities as everyone else. And that day, if the damn bill ever passes, is now just a little bit closer.

December, 2013

But You *CAN'T* Be Her Mother

'Are you a boy or a girl?' Now that my daughter is turning six, I'm starting to get this question regularly from her classmates. Usually they sidle up, a little self-consciously because they've heard something (that I'm trying to pass myself off as female and her mother), and they want to check it out; but also to put me back in my place if it's true.

With men who taunt me like this on the street, I can respond by asking in reply, "Are you an asshole or an idiot?" With the six-year-old boy who is rolling his eyes right now as I try to affirm that I'm Dylan's mom, this is clearly not an appropriate response.

Nor, as I might have done in earlier years, can I threaten to picket the school—or perhaps just the first-grade class to which he belongs—to protest this *blatant display of transphobia.*

In fact, all the in-your-face tricks I learned to counter intolerance fail me now. What to do when you're a Transexual Menace faced with a pint-sized harasser who barely comes up to your navel? What to do when gender bigotry is aimed as much at your little daughter as you? Menace-ing a six-year-old is not the way to go. Especially since he's not so much asking a question as making a statement, to wit: I've heard you're trying to pass yourself off as a girl and Dylan's mom, and I want to confirm it firsthand so I can tell you that you're not really a girl or a mother.

These are questions I never had to address. It strikes me now that being a parent dramatically enlarges your zone of vulnerability, while at the same time shrinking your range of response. And, to be frank, at the moment I just feel humiliated and vaguely ridiculous here on the playground.

None of which I can explain to this little twerp. I can't even explain my genderqueerness, since this is not the time for an in-depth discussion of transsexuality complete with before and after pictures and detailed surgical diagrams which his parents—not to mention the principal—would not appreciate.

Whatever I do, I better do it quick, because my little daughter is staring at me, looking for a hint as to how to handle this. And here is it: I've spend decades learning to accept myself, but I've never wanted so badly to be cisgendered, to be an RG (a "real girl"), as I do right now. I want to spare this for my daughter.

And, yet, at the same time, I don't. I not only want her to understand gender difference, I hope—in my own small, clumsy, distinctly non-activist-y way— that I'm even modeling it for her. As my wife and I fight the onslaught of impossibly small-waisted, tippy-toed Barbie dolls, the omnipresent Disney princess toys of every size, shape and description, and the Pink Plague of gifts that descends on her like a veil every birthday and Christmas, part of me fervently hopes that *my* little RG will find ways to be other-gendered. I want her not to buy into the narrow, confining feminine stereotypes that will claim many of her peers. She doesn't have to be a dyke; Lord, but couldn't she at least be a little bit of a tomboy?

Usually, after these little episodes with her friends, the big bad gender activist slinks off and licks her (his?) wounds in private. But not this time. Not this morning. As soon as I get home, I write the following and send it to the entire school diversity staff. I'm quite sure this is the opening shot in what will be a much longer conflict. Perhaps I'm finally figuring out a way to be a trans activist parent after all:

This morning the fourth or fifth child in one of Dylan's classes in the last couple of years has asked me if I was a really a boy or a girl. I think honest questions, even ones which may be awkward or personal, should always be welcomed from a child. But this is seldom asked to obtain information, or to clarify a point about which a child—to be frank— might reasonably be expected to be confused.

Whatever the answer, I'm informed that I really do look like a boy, or that I can't really be Dylan's mom. Often this is right in front of Dyl. The "really" is instructive; the point is not information, but to police gender lines and particularly to stigmatize gender difference. This usually leaves Dyl in a bad space, trying to decide whether to defend me as her mom or else let it go among kids she will, after all, have to coexist with in class every day.

In a couple of cases, this scenario has played out in my absence directly with Dylan, with pretty much the same result. In a sense, it's not too much different from asking the child of two moms or two dads which one is "really" their parent.

Although, given my interaction with the school, I should know by now, I confess I'm still a bit unclear how much or how little of the DC Public Schools current anti-bullying curriculum addresses issues of gender, and at what age it does so.

In any case, gender constancy—the conception that gender is fixed and that bodies are rigidly defined between male and female—begins to take hold right around age 5 or 6. It is also around this time that harassment against kids who are gender nonconforming or even (more rarely) cross-gender, begins to take root in earnest.

Based on my own experience, it might make sense to begin addressing gender intolerance in their diversity and anti-bullying lessons in greater depth at this age, since whatever education they are currently getting, if any, is clearly not enough.

No DCPS parent should have to be repeatedly mocked in front of their own child—and certainly no DCPS child should have to stand by and watch their parent be ridiculed—simply because he or she is gender different and that children have the idea that this sort of prejudice, unlike those based on race, sexual orientation, or religion, is a socially acceptable basis for intolerance, teasing or ridicule. Thank you. Riki

December, 2013

Transgender Dinosaurs and the Rise of the Genderqueers

She was a lovely 13-year-old girl with long blond hair, bright hazel eyes, and the budding bosom and hips of the woman she would soon be. Her flashing smile betrayed none of the self-consciousness that I had when I was young and began—as a transsexual—dressing in feminine clothing. I assumed she was a friend of the young transwoman I was there to meet, and while I searched for her, I ignored this young woman because it was obviously simply impossible to see her as anything but a woman.

Never having passed as female, as I'd grown older I'd finally given up trying. Besides, it seemed somehow counter-revolutionary. The new transgender politics was increasingly built around exactly the kind prominent social visibility and defiant non-passing that my Cleveland Clinic doctors had assured me would signal both my "failure" as a transsesxual and of their efforts to turn me into a woman.

In fact, my political identity for 30 years has been built around and on the foundation of my being visibly transgender—from the day I donned a Transexual Menace NYC T-shirt and flew to the Brandon Teena murder trial in Falls City, NE.

Memorial vigils for slain transgender women, picketing HRC, books on gender theory and public fights with radical feminists, and even being booted— more than once—out of the Michigan Womyn's Music Festival for not being a "born womyn": who and what I am is inextricably intertwined with being a visible transsexual.

But what if all that were wiped away? Who would I be? What would I have become? Unlike society's unwritten rule—"prove you're really a woman"—Nature's rule is "female, unless proven otherwise." In utero we are all females. It is only through the action of testosterone in the womb and beyond that, that slightly fewer than half of us develop into those "other females"—men.

Androgen blockers, which prevent all the painful and irrevocable pubertal effects of testosterone, and which I would spend several years of my life trying to reverse—chest hair, beard, Adam's apple, etc.—had made this young person into an entirely non-transgender transsexual, one whose gender, whose social identity, will be always be completely female to every adult she knows or meets. With the right surgeon, she might never tell her husband, or wife. She didn't cross gender lines or even rub up against them. This is not to say that she will never experience any of the pain or dislocation I felt, or that (like many trans youth) she will not voluntarily live out and open, anyway. But she has the option of a kind of social acceptance and life opportunity which make me very glad for her, even though they are ones of which I could only dream.

In my adolescence it was unthinkable to even mention being transgender to my parents or doctors, let alone seek treatment. And treatment, if it was forthcoming at all, would have inevitably meant psychiatrists (not to mention having my father try to beat me into manhood, a project he'd already started).

Blockers are something akin to the life-saving anti-retroviral cocktails that abruptly and astonishingly banished the public, visible effects of HIV for so many people overnight. As androgen blockers are increasingly taken by adolescents whose parents are more supportive and protective than I can imagine, we are in danger of suddenly and abruptly banishing the public transsexual.

And I don't mean only that in a generation or two we may become invisible in the public space, which one could argue is a positive or a negative thing. Rather, I mean that in ten years the entire *experience* we understand today as constituting transgender—the political advocacy, support groups, literature, theory and books that have come to define it since transgender burst from its closet in the early 1990s to become part of the LGB-and-now-T movement—all that may be vanishing. In 50 years it might be as if we never existed. Our memories, our accomplishments, our political movement, will all seem historic and antique. Feeling transgender will not so much become more acceptable, as gayness is now doing, but logically impossible. In other words, I may be a gender dinosaur without knowing it.

Which is exactly how this young girl makes me

feel as she smiles and walks past me in a sky blue summer dress I think I was born too old to wear, and out onto the sunlit sidewalk where a young man turns to look at her and then smile. I'm reminded at this moment that the dinosaurs—who once ruled all—had no warning that their extinction was around the corner.

Which way begs yet another common (and unkind) straight question: if every gay person could take a pill that would make them heterosexual, would they take it? That may be an ancient and homophobic hypothetical for gay people. But the question of blockers—if you could take pill that would make you not transgender, would you take it?—is now a real possibility for every young trannie with understanding parents.

And here's another hypothetical, in its own way even tougher: if this adolescent was *your* child, would you let her take hormone blockers? Would you want for her the experience of visibility, ostracism, and harassment—along with all the positive benefits, like pearls from oysters, for the luckier of us—or the permanent disappearing act and normalcy the blockers now hold out?

These are the sorts of questions no minority has had to answer, until now.

In fact, gay people never needed a pill. Most of them could disappear simply by refusing to "act gay," which meant toning down the camp and gender displays and passing as straight, as gay people have done for thousands of years to survive in deeply homophobic and dangerous societies. Public and highly visible queerness was not a necessity for homosexuals in anything like the way it's been for tranwomen .

But there has always been that foundational and private residue of gayness that remains: attraction to the same sex, which can be suppressed or hidden, but not disappeared.

For the blocker babies, there is no residue. Their transgender-ness is there, and then—poof!—it's gone. If there was an anti-gay pill, perhaps today no one would take it because to be gay is no longer to suffer in anything like the same degree or dimension as just 30 years ago.

But will transgender ever be as accepted? And even supposing it is, will we have to wait another 30 years, or 40 or 50? And even supposing acceptance comes, will it ever be as good as simply being able to be a woman without a pronoun, modifier, or asterisk?

What makes this question more remarkable is that the rise of the blocker babies comes just as transgender is finding a new and stronger voice among young people. Genderqueerness is enjoying a surprising popularity , now with national and local organizations that are highly sophisticated, media savvy, and staffed with real professionals.

More youth are enjoying queering identities, doing versions of non-male and non-female, and all sorts of gender drag in between, that both mock binary genders and threaten to turn them inside out. Many of these new kinds of transpeople are located in a space beyond the hormones-and-surgery route I took.

Perhaps the better question is not "will transsexuality go the way of the dinos?" but rather, "Are we entering a new age of 'Born This Way' public genderqueerness that exists alongside it?"

Big, Schlumpy White Guys Cast as Transwomen

In "Transgender, Schlumpy, and Human," Jennifer Finny Boylan's recent *New York Times* column ponders why the new Amazon show, *Transparent* (on which she consulted) had to feature a MTF transgender lead played by Jeffrey Tambor, a large, schlumpy cisgender male (for the non-Yiddish among us, Urban Dictionary defines "schlumpy" as unkempt, rumpled, road worn, and sloppy—qualities every woman hopes to embody).

Yet she confesses to be won over by the show's "charm... grace and respect," asserting that the use of a "schlumpy, older person rather than a gorgeous [transgender] fashion model is good for both trans and cis folks alike."

Yeah, right.

Apparently Boylan has never seen HBO's *Normal,* which (wait for it)... featured a large, schlumpy, older male Tom Wilkerson as a MTF transgender woman.

Or Priscilla, *Queen of the Desert*, which featured a large, schlumpy, older male, Terrance Stamp, as an MTF transgender woman.

Or *Kiss of the Spider Woman*, (William Hurt, ditto)

Or *The World According to Garp*, (John Lithgow, still ditto)... etc., etc., ad nauseam.

Is it just me, or is a subtle pattern developing here?

We are much more likely to be played by big-boned, worn, older cisgender males than anyone else. The worn, cisgender male playing trans serves several important entertainment functions for the cisgender audience.

First, what could be more poignant and funny than for old, tall, broad-shouldered guys like Tambor, Hurt, Lithgow, Wilkerson, or Stamp to announce to the audience that he's "really a woman?"

Second, this kind of casting reinforces the worst kind of biological essentialism (some would now call it "cis-sexism") that is the defining feature of cisgender views about us, and thus presumably of cisgender viewers. You can see this playing out in real-time on the recent *Piers Morgan Show* and *Katie*, where interviews of transgender actresses focused on their genitalia and sensationalize their birth sex.

Transgender people must never be seen as simply "normal." We can never be more than the sum of the changes we've made to our bodies and we must always appear as visibly, comfortably, reliably different. After all, what would be the point of casting a transgender character if they looked just like you or me? Well, you, anyway.

(This reminds me of my days at GenderPAC, when media people at our events would ask me to find someone for their photographers to shoot "who looks more transgender.")

Finally, casting this recurring parade of similar actors avoids the deep confusion and male rage with which male viewers would respond if they were ever presented with a sexy female character who turned them on... and then turned out to be an MTF.

At all costs, transwomen characters must *never* be sexy. I mean, imagine young guys sharing a beer together while watching a hot, scantily dressed actress on a show, maybe joke about what she would look like naked or what she's like in bed, and then... she's a trannie! My god, that would light up the Twitter-verse with outraged males feeling *punked.* Well, with tall old bald Tambor or Hurt or Lithgow or Stamp or Wilkerson there's no chance of *that* happening.

One of the few exceptions, besides the wonderful Laverne Cox in *Orange is the New Black*, was Lisa Edelstein's transsexual character on *Ally McBeal*, or maybe Jaye Davidson as Dil in *The Crying Game.* Then again, every time Edelstein was on, the show's writers found new ways to have one character or another blurt out the word *penis* in front of her as an ongoing punchline.

(Exclaiming the word *penis* is *very* funny when said in the presence of a transgender woman.)

And in the Crying Game, Dil's cisgender lover vomits violently (and punches out her lights) after discovering she's trans. Maybe not such exceptions there after all.

I find none of this the slightest bit charming or entertaining.

The characters and the casting are stigmatizing, demeaning, and patronizing in the worst. I couldn't give a crap how well Tambor (a comedic actor whose modest talents escape me) impersonates a transgender woman in *Transparent*.

We are still being played for tokens: edgy characters from well-intentioned shows to attract progressive viewers by showing how charming our life struggles can be, meanwhile keeping us within narrow, expected boundaries that don't threaten cisgender viewers or their need to always think of us as pathetic, strange, inevitably masculine, and basically male.

Makes me want to go out and rent Ticked Off Trannies With Knives (2010). After all, we get to play us, we don't charm anyone, and in the end there's not a single old male schlump left standing.

RadFems and TERFS

Michelle Goldberg's *New Yorker* piece "What is a Woman?" is remarkable for what it says and what it doesn't say. It details the trials and tribulations of self-described RadFems against transactivists and their allies. Apparently it's becoming difficult for Radical Fems to participate in polite society.

Radical feminists cling to notions of biological essentialism: that there is a common core experience that all cisgender women share, and that transwomen can never participate in this experience, and thus are now, and always will be, males.

It's not exactly clear when kicking the political crap out of trannies became either "radical," or even "feminist," but it probably originated 40 years ago with Janice Raymond's book *The Transsexual Empire.* That initiated a period in my life in the 1980s and 90s when it was virtually impossible for me to attend any lesbian or women's event without someone bringing up that book and its noxious arguments. A long, impassioned debate about me and the meaning of my body and my attendance would ensue, often by very well-intentioned women, which, as often as not, would end in my being publicly asked, or told, to leave.

This kind of debate is pretty much the same trick Michelle pulls off in this piece. She quotes both sides at length, being very well-intentioned in moderating the "debate," as if the arguments put forth are equally valid, and neither she, nor *The New Yorker*, need take sides. Her tone is one of utter moral passivity.

In effect, it's precisely kind of article that would have been run 20 years ago about gays and lesbians. It would have quoted homophobic bigots saying that homosexuality was a disease and/or a lifestyle choice, and gay rights activists saying otherwise, and both sides would have been given equal treatment.

In other words, this article is—in its quiet, quasi-liberal, intelligentsia way—nearly as transphobic and bigoted as the RadFems whose trials it covers. And these trials are the second interesting thing about the piece. Radfems are finding themselves on the wrong end of history.

An ever-dwindling segment of polite society is willing to continue refusing to acknowledge transgender people. We're not exactly taking the courts by storm, like gay marriage, but we're definitely on an upswing here. "Normal"—might be just around the next few corners—who knows?

As a result, RadFems are going through, well, pretty much exactly the kind of thing I did 20 years ago. Every time they show up at an event, particularly at lesbian or women's groups, someone brings up RadFem's noxious arguments. A long, impassioned debate about them and the meaning of their positions and attendance ensues, often by very well-intentioned women, and often ending with them being asked (or told) to leave.

Even Raymond herself is now being disinvited to, and barred from events. Does the long arc of the moral universe bends towards justice, or what? Today's truly *radical* feminism is being waged by young people who see transgender rights as co-extensive with theirs.

For example, when a Quaker college refused to acknowledge the transition of a young FTM, insisting that he was still female, student protesters repeatedly turned out to protest the decision, and have dogged the administration's every step. They picketed with signs that read, among other things, "Trans Rights Are Feminist Rights." When I read that it took my breath away.

The trans-haters aren't done yet by any means, but the tables are turning. Trans-phobes are set to become the new trannies. Watch what you wish for. What goes around comes around. Yes, it does take nearly forever. Revenge really is a dish served cold. But it does come around.

Now, will someone please pass me a plate of cold RadFem revenge?

February, 2015

Equinox Genderfuck

For those who've never heard of it, *Equinox* is a high-end luxury gym that prides itself on being a cutting edge, overtly friendly, one-stop shop for those wanting to knock their bods back into shape. Alas, it's also pretty much the only gym left in sunny, gay South Beach. There's Crunch, but the less said about that one the better.

It didn't used to be like this. For one thing, gay South Beach used to be well... actually gay. When I bought my first closet-sized condo so I would avoid some of the worst of New York's winters, there were five body-building gyms within walking distance: David Barton, Iron Works, etc. None offered yoga or aerobics, or any of those other "faggy," lifestyle classes.

All were mostly gay, as was the neighborhood. South Beach had once been a quiet Cuban enclave with lots of Hasidic Jews. Until gay men discovered it in the late 80s and helped set off rounds of gentrification that continue today, it was a neighborhood of old Orthodox synagogues that has now become an enclave of new condos.

The gay muscle queens would walk, often hand in hand, to their favorite gyms in the morning to work out, just as the Orthodox men in their fur lined hats would walk to their shuls to pray at sunset.

More than a few of these gay men were impossibly beefed up—totally ripped to the tits on steroids that helped counter the deleterious effects of the new HIV cocktails that were suddenly returning them, unbelievably, to life.

But all that is gone. *Equinox* is pretty straight, as far as I can tell. Even the cute trainers with the tight butts are straight. And yet, like South Beach itself, it's still strangely laid-back and tolerant in a way that few communities can match—unlike clubs in Greenwich Village and Dupont Circle, both of which I'd lived in for decades.

One of the things *Equinox* does to maintain its hip, upscale yuppie cred is roll out MTV-style videos at all their gyms, edgy-ish but often simply perplexing, with the theme "Equinox made me do it."

Last week I noticed their newest offering on the big video board at the entrance. First, a masked muscle-builder gets spray painted. A bearded man cradles fountain in which a stone baby emits water instead of pee. Then a striking, long-haired blond model struts and pouts for the camera before taking off her coat to reveal her… bare, flat, manly chest.

In the early days of GenderPAC, we couldn't even get HRC to say 'LGBT.' Gay newspapers wouldn't cover transgender news, and politicians of all sorts, other than those in the Bay Area, ran from trans issues.

Now we're in Netflix and Amazon TV series,

HRC can't live without us, and even the President says "LGBT." And *Equinox*, the upscale gym chain straight yuppies crave, is putting genderfuck front and center in its latest national branding campaign. Good genderfuck, too (I'm a bit of a connoisseur in this narrow realm). In fact, it was so well done that I used my phone to video it and screened it for my daughter ("Cool!"). This is what social progress looks like.

In South Beach I wonder if anyone notices. When we moved down here and enrolled our daughter, DJ, in school, we were more than a little worried. Even at our very small, personal school in DC, she and I had both been taunted and teased by the kids over my being transgender. This school was huge—easily four times as large—and we were total outsiders who knew no one.

I made sure to wear a skirt to morning drop-off every other day of DJ's first week of school. I thought we might as well get the harassment out in the open and deal with it. I plotted how to approach the principal, how she'd react when I complained, and how far I could press my points.

I needn't have bothered. It may not have as many gays as it used to, but South Beach still retains its famous get-along, laid-back attitude. No one said anything. All the PTA parents shook our hands or hugged us hello.

The only exception was one boy in DJ's class. He asked her who was her dad. DJ replied she didn't have a dad, she had two moms. "Then who's that guy who in a dress who drops you off?" he teased her. "She transgender, dude! Get over it!" Now that's MY daughter.

June, 2015

Trans Is Beautiful

By now, you, like everyone else, has seen the incredible "After" *Vanity Fair* picture of Caitlyn Jenner. Then again, if Annie Leibovitz was photographing me, I'd probably look like Eva Peron.

Her picture points up two uncomfortable truths about being a transgender woman. First, for the most part, we look different. If you're a trans man you can counter many of the more unfortunate effects of estrogen by taking testosterone: growing body hair, getting a deeper voice, having bigger muscles. It doesn't work the other way around. Once you have a deep voice, a six-foot frame and wide shoulders, no amount of estrogen is going to undo that.

By denying us hormones, or at least hormone blockers --when we're young, society allows us to be poisoned by our own bodies. They don't even have to do anything; they simply have to *not* do anything. This is currently the experience of the vast majority of us, and that is why most of us do not look like Caitlyn Jenner.

You can address some of the facial effects through feminization surgery, getting a nose job (guilty as charged), Adam's apple shave (ditto), cheek reshaping and sanding down of heavy eyebrows (nope). But the fact of transitioning for a transwoman from male-to-female is that your body's basic chassis is going to stay pretty much the same.

This brings us to the second uncomfortable truth about being a transgender woman, which is that we have allowed ourselves to be thoroughly colonized by cisgender aesthetics. We let cisgender women set the standards by which we are judged and often judge ourselves. If Caitlyn had ended up looking like Lea DeLaria, I doubt she would have gotten the pin-up cover photo in *Vanity Fair*.

We grow up marinated in a culture which despises transgender bodies and tries its best to teach us to do the same. Well, few of us are born hoping to look genderqueer. Yet, in the 1970s, African-Americans were able to challenge the dominant white aesthetics of straight hair, light skin, and tiny noses through campaigns declaring that *Black Is Beautiful!*

Decades ago when I transitioned, people complimented me by saying "You look just like a real woman!" Even today, people still say that to me when they intend a compliment.

At a national conference of executives last week, one attendee went out of her way to explain she had "never suspected" that I was transgender. This, of course, was high praise. Looking transgender is apparently some kind of failure. Certainly she would have been dismayed and insulted if I'd told her that I had suspected she was trans.

Cisgender people pull this kind of crap all the time, and they will continue until we start pushing back. As a movement we've waited far too long to mount a full-on, frontal assault on cisgender aesthetic standards, and their colonization of our bodies and our minds.

There are many ways of being beautiful in this world. Not every one of us will look like Caitlyn or Janet Mock. But we don't need to. Next time a cisgender person tells you they never suspected you were transgender, tell them with a smile: "Get your standards off my body. Hey, trans is beautiful!"

May, 2016

The (Coming) Nonbinary Revolution

There has been a lot written lately about transpeople in bathrooms, mostly courtesy of the right wing's continuing obsession with a toxic amalgam of biological essentialism, sexual panic over adolescent innocence, and the just-won't-die meme of genderqueers as potential predators. *Mea culpa.*

Much of the debate has focused on stories like that of 16-year-old transman Gavin Grimm, who, with others, is suing the Gloucester County, VA, school board, seeking access to the appropriate bathroom that matches their gender identity. The ACLU, the Department of Education, HRC, and others are rightfully seeking to support such students in gaining access to the appropriate (binary) Boys or Girls rooms.

Completely overlooked in this debate (except by the *UK Guardian*) is the more incendiary case of 20-year-old Maria Munir, a student who addressed President Obama during a town hall in London. Maria, terrified of the reaction that might ensue, but forcing hirself forward, publicly informed the President that s/he was a nonbinary person.

Think about that: not as a *boi*, or one of the *girlz,* or as transmale or transfemale, but Off the Freakin' Binary.

Since then, Maria has reported receiving an unexpected outpouring of support—which is wonderful. But the challenges posed by hir self-outing have been almost half a century in the making, and they are profound. They cut to the heart of arguments that trans-advocates and their allies have been making for some time in the face of furious right wing opposition to trans-identity generally, and to the "boys in the Girls Room," specifically.

We might simplify the main thrust of this challenge in two basic points:

First, as a matter of simple human dignity, transpeople should be allowed to access the bathroom that fits their gender identity. Full stop.

Second, as a strictly practical matter, if we enforce the strict birth-certificate biological essentialism the right-wing demands, we'll end up with masculine-appearing male-identified people who live as men in the Women's Room, and feminine appearing female-identified people who live as women in the Men's Room, which is a ridiculous result for public policy.

Maria (and others like hir) are set to completely confound both of these arguments. Gay and transgender rights advocates have been quietly dodging the issue of binary heteronormativity, but that sound you hear is the other shoe finally dropping... hard.

As to the first argument, there *is* no "appropriate" bathroom which legal advocates might fight for Maria to access because the argument depends on fitting Maria into the dominant, hetero-binary structure of boy/girl. Those of us who are profoundly genderqueer have had to struggle with this since birth).

Simply put, in Maria's case, there is no underlying binary gender identification on which to base the claim. You have to, instead, critique the hetero-binary structure itself.

Almost all the cases I'm familiar with refute the right-wing's hysterical cry of "boys will invade girls' restrooms!" because of individuals who showed some degree of consonance between their gender identity and usual notions of masculinity or femininity. This is why it was unexceptional to hear Donald Trump say that if Caitlyn Jenner visited Trump Tower she could use any bathroom she wanted, presumably including the Women's Room. One can scarcely imagine her doing anything else, which is why the lack of a ring-wing outcry was the dog that didn't bark.

But what happens when a genderqueer individual who genuinely looks and sounds profoundly nonbinary, and/or masculine, declares in a binary world s/he would be most comfortable accessing the girl's restroom? To say the least, the optics would no longer work. Nor would appeals to practicality. What really needs to be contested here is not just our right to use bathrooms with dignity (which would, personally, be very welcome), but the entire underlying hetero-binary structuring of the world that queers must inhabit.

This is the real struggle, and queer activists have been talking about it at least since the 1970s Gay Liberation movement, even as the movement it spawned has continued to nudge it aside.

All of which is to say, transgender advocates and their allies are doing good work, but they have finally, and perhaps unwittingly, opened the gender Pandora's Box, and over the next few years all sorts of unexpected nonbinary things, like Maria, will come popping out. This is going to be interesting.

Burn Down the Binary!

June, 2016

Mommy's About to Be Normal

There will be a lot written about the new fight between the Department of Justice and the state of North Carolina over transgender bathroom access. My own response (besides briefly tearing up) was to ask my nine-year-old daughter to put down her iPhone long enough to watch the nationwide press conference by the DOJ.

I explained the Attorney General to her as the top lawyer and policeman in the country. I explained what she was saying by telling her, "Remember this moment: Mommy's about to be normal." I then called all the people who helped me start GenderPAC back in 1994.

It was 1995 when the DOJ hate crimes staff agreed to a first meeting on trans issues. I was so sick I said nothing, and was literally falling off my chair, at times. But I knew it was the start of something, and I had to be there. So, yes, it took 21 years. But, yes, we are all about to finally be normal.

There is a lot of nuance here that will go largely unmentioned in all the commentary to come. So let me hold a few things up to the light.

First of all, we *are* about to be normal. I mean

that in two ways. To begin with, this was as big a line in the sand as any of us could have wished for. The federal government just announced that it is putting its full weight and authority behind the proposition that transgender people are legitimate, and transgender rights must be respected.

The second way is in what was *not* said. The DOJ did not justify this on the grounds that we have a mental diagnosis (i.e., Gender Identity Disorder) that must be respected. In fact, even Ted Cruz, who ran truly vile adds in the Indiana Republican primary attacking Donald Trump for his tolerance of transgender bathroom access, did not attack us as being deranged or otherwise suffering from a psychiatric condition (which in any case should not be stigmatized anyway).

The right wing in general, and Mr. Cruz specifically, have also pretty much avoided attacking us as immoral. In fact, few of the right-wing bigots transfixed by trans issues have availed themselves of their favorite new argument to hold back the tide on gay rights: to wit, that religious conviction grants them the right not to serve us, marry us, bake wedding cakes for us, or photograph us, because doing so would violate their moral beliefs.

On the contrary, both Mr. Cruz and his ilk (and of course the DOJ) have addressed this strictly as a matter of rights (the right to privacy vs. trans civil rights). I realize this is a small thing and truly cold comfort, but that's what *normal* looks like, when it starts to break out.

This brings me to the biggest thing about the press conference. Attorney General Loretta Lynch and the head of her Civil Rights Division, Vanita Gupta, just denounced transgender discrimination by putting it on a par with Jim Crow, that pernicious system of discrimination that—besides denying them the right to vote—consigned decades of African Americans (mainly in the South) to separate and inferior bathrooms, drinking fountains, classrooms, buses, train seats, etc., thereby condemning many of them to no public accommodations whatsoever when separate ones were unavailable.

LGBT advocates have often mined the historical parallels, some facile and some thoughtful, between gay rights and the Black civil rights movement. It has often proven a contentious issue.

But to see this argument being made by an African-American woman—indeed by two women of color—about discrimination against transgender people is profound. It is the sound of a door closing on a particular era and a particular kind of bigotry that perhaps not my children, but certainly their children, will never be burdened with knowing.

Which brings me back to *normal* and the underlying arguments—the silent aspects of the position they're taking. The Achilles Heel of transgender rights has always been that our bodies are employed to testify against us. Like pain or religious experience, my gender identity is something only I can know with certainty. But my birth sex and genitals can and always have been read against me to undermine my political pursuit of my own rights.

So to take a position radically in favor of transgender rights like the DOJ did today is to say: Whether we can see it or not, even if what we see tells us otherwise, we, as a society, will respect what this person tells us about their identity and experience. And we are willing to put the full weight and credit of proper society behind your right to live in dignity and respect with those feelings wherever they take you, and as long as you harm no one else in their pursuit.

This is, in its own quiet way, an extraordinary leap of faith in the human soul. This is what happened at today's news conference. There will be intersex, and nonbinary, and other rights to come. And there will be more legal thrashing from the right wing as it fights a losing rearguard battle.

But tramspeopole and genderqueers became legitimate today. Mark your calendars. Because of it tomorrow's gender nonconforming children will grow up in a different world.

February, 2017

Approximately Beautiful

I love that in this cultural moment when we're fixated on bathrooms, Laverne Cox is taking on the issue of transgender beauty, as detailed in a recent *Daily Beast* article.

Regarding the rallying cry "Trans is Beautiful," Laverne explained: "All the things that make me uniquely and beautifully trans—my big hands, my big feet, my wide shoulders, my deep voice—all of these things are beautiful. I'm not beautiful despite these things. I'm beautiful because of them."

Actually, no.

It's a brave and wonderful thing to say, but it's simply not true. Laverne and Janet and Caitlin are considered "beautiful" by the dominant cultural precisely because they *do* tend to fit in with cisgender aesthetic standards. And the cis-ies love this stuff, as Cox showed in her nude spread for *Allure* magazine. Even *French Vogue* is featuring a transgender model on the cover of its current issue.

To the degree that we approximate them they are willing to consider us attractive (and sadly, too many of us are willing to consider ourselves by those same standards). As Laverne noted when she explained that fans who call her gorgeous really mean "that in certain lighting, at certain angles, I am able to embody certain cis-normative beauty standards....[ones which] many trans folks will never be able to embody."

The emergence of a truly transgender aesthetic, a way of valuing profoundly genderqueer bodies, does not seem visible on the horizon. The malevolence of the cisgender aesthetic is nearly universal. Almost every transperson experiences it at some point, some of us daily. At times it is actively toxic—when we are called *freaks*, snickered at because of our looks, or publicly calling out as that "dude in a dress."

All of this is meant to make us ashamed of how we look, which means being ashamed of not looking like *them*. Just as often, this hegemony is casually poisonous while superficially tolerant: for instance, the women at my gym who look away when I enter the changing room; those in my yoga class who pointedly look right through me but smile to acknowledge other women.

No, I *don't* look like you. I shouldn't need to. It even takes the form of the cis-ies' never-ending pronoun assaults on transpeople—not just repeatedly referring to us by the wrong pronoun (and of course never bothering to inquire about the correct one), but sometimes even continuing to use the wrong one, even when we correct them.

This kind of behavior is not organized, but it is intentional. This is what a culture looks like when it polices its own standards against those who threaten it. It ostracizes, it ridicules, and it insistently mislabels.

At every juncture, it controls and owns the discourse about attractiveness. It is up to us to fit in.

These are tactics also used by the dominant culture with people of color, or people who identify as fat, those bodies who are differently abled—in fact the entire aesthetic zoo of those of us outside traditional standards of "attractiveness."

Alas, no, Laverne, I don't think that what you call your "big hands," "big feet," and "wide shoulders" are why the cis-ies find you lovely. I think it is largely in spite of them. The fact that you even have to list these attributes shows that they are neither accepted nor acceptable. You may find yourself lovely because of them, and I might as well, but I doubt your cisgender audience does.

It is no accident that three outspoken women who have emerged as our community spokestrans at this moment can all be seen as fitting conventional cisgender standards of beauty. I love that they look how they do. I honor it, along with their bravery, courage, and political chops. But I do not mistake their popularity for the emergence of a transgender-friendly aesthetic.

We will know it happens when actors who look visibly, undeniably genderqueer are front and center. Perhaps unsurprisingly, most of those who are just beginning to emerge in this space are seen as trans-males who, like model Rain Dove, have "softer" features, thus are less threatening to mainstream audiences (and it doesn't hurt to have cheekbones even God would kill for).

I think it's helpful to continue to name and shame what we're up against. I track what cis-ies present as absurd and ridiculous when it comes to gendered bodies, because such images are highly instructive of the boundaries of their aesthetic tolerance, and what places they simply will and will not let transpeople go.

One telling example was widely disseminated by Hooters in its campaign to highlight why they should not be sued for sex discrimination for not hiring males. They used a very hairy, heavyset man posed seductively in short-shorts and plunging neckline to make what I'm sure they thought was a killing point: what could be more ridiculous, even revolting? This is the kind of perpetual and quietly malevolent gender warfare that cisgender culture enacts against trans self-respect and self-acceptance every day.

So, yes, they let a few of us in. But the rest of us—who are profoundly genderqueer, who go well beyond the boundaries of any possible cisgender notions of attractiveness, who refuse to go back in the closet or to try to pass, and who challenge the aesthetic standards not only imposed upon us, but used to shame and degrade us—we struggle every day to have whatever quiet sort of elusive beauty we might possess acknowledged.

It's a long road ahead, and no end in sight.

March, 2017

"Billions" of Genders: They, Them, & Theirs

"Hello sir, my name is Taylor. My pronouns are they, theirs, and them."

For years I fought a running battle with many of the current leadership of the transgender movement. They were committed to trans-only identity politics for the basis for the movement. I wanted not only to open up the politics to include LGB people, but move beyond that towards genderqueerness.

I lost. It wasn't even close. The movement moved on. I was at least two decades ahead of schedule. I coined the term "genderqueer" back in the 1990s in an effort to glue together two nouns which seemed to me to describe an excluded and overlooked middle: those of us who were not only queer, but were so because we were the kind of gendertrash society rejected.

A prominent gay columnist immediately attacked me in print for "ruining a perfectly good word like *queer*." (Harrumph!) Joan Nestle, Clare Howell, and I then used the word for the title of our anthology of emerging young writers (*GenderQueer: Voices from*

Beyond the Binary, 2002). But, I don't think anyone expected the term or the concept to catch on.

Then one year I was attending the Creating Change conference (the year's biggest queer youth event), and using the (wonderfully gender-neutral) bathrooms. I saw someone had posted a sticker on the wall that read, "A Genderqueer Was Here!" I thought, "Hmm... that's really interesting. Someone is using that not as a descriptor, but as the basis for their identity." So it begins.

Fast forward only four years, and I was reading Matt Bernstein's anthology (*Nobody Passes: Rejecting the Rules of Gender and Conformity,* 2006), and in it writer Rocko Bulldagger bemoans the term's very existence, declaring, "I am sick to death of hearing it." Such is the arc of a new idea.

But if your eyes were open, you could see this coming a long way off. At Camp Trans outside the Michigan Womyn's Music Festival every year, I'd meet one young person after another who were calling themselves simply "boychik," "demigirl," "transmasculine," "tryke," and any number of exuberant genders few of us had contemplated. Camp Trans itself was always overrun by one set of teens and 20-somethings, explaining patiently—if in exasperation—to ardently les-fem mothers (who'd brought them along to experience the beauty of womanhood) that they needed to move beyond their transphobia and accept the transwomen at Michigan *as* women. They were amplified by another group of teens and 20-somethings who were not explaining much of anything to anyone, but were busily and joyously destroying the entire idea of men and women, sexual orientation and gender identity, by simply trampling over any binary identity or boundary they could find.

We've spent almost 40 years fighting for a bunch of identity categories which are based entirely on the implicit acceptance that there are two and only two basic sexes, with the associated possible gender identities and sexual orientations that come from them. Now young people are about to blow all that up.

I was reminded of this while watching Showtime's hit TV show *Billions*, which introduced a new character, Taylor, whose gender I was having fun trying to puzzle out. Taylor is an intense, over-brilliant intern who wears a shirt and tie and a buzz-crewcut, but otherwise has no identifiable landmarks by which the viewer might navigate the gender terrain.

Finally, they are introduced to Bobby Axelrod, the head of multi-billion dollar hedge fund Axe Capital. As played by Asia Kate Dillon, they reply: *"Hello sir, my name is Taylor. My pronouns are 'they, theirs, and them.'"* Cutting edge stuff, and a signpost for where the gender dialog is going.

In a recent article at *Refinery29* Dillon explained that as they read the part, "I did some research into nonbinary, and I just thought, 'Oh my gosh, like, that's me... that's who I am.' When I read the script for episode two and I saw the '*they, theirs* and *them*,' that's when the tears started to well up in my eyes. Then when I read Axe's response, which is, 'Okay,' and then the scene just continues, that's what ultimately moved me to full-fledged tears."

This is powerful stuff. And it's only the start. The trans movement is going to have to accommodate and open the boundaries perhaps more than it would like.

But if it's the job of young people to expose and explode their elders' paradigm, these young people are off to a wonderful start.

"Hello. My name is Riki. My pronouns are they, theirs, and them."

March, 2017

All About My Mother

It was a month ago that my mother died. She was 92 and it was painless and brief, and I was grateful for that. My feelings for her have always been deeply conflicted. Why did she stand by and allow our father to savage us so? My father only wanted strong, manly, athletic young sons, and ended up getting none of them. As a result, he produced three stunted offspring.

How could my mother be so ashamed of me when I transitioned that she tried to hide my existence from the neighbors for years? As Oscar Wilde said, "Children begin by loving their parents; as they grow older they judge them; sometimes they forgive them."

When you're little, a parent is your entire world. You expect almost nothing from them, and you accept almost anything from them. A parent's love, if you're lucky enough to get it, is a little bit of God, as close to the transcendent as most of us will ever get.

So we don't mind their shortcomings, as long as they give love and acceptance. Unfortunately, this is something many transpeople have grown up without. So we hold on to our anger. We want them to come around, to at last give the love they have withheld. In my case, as in so many others, it never comes.

Without ever consciously thinking it, every parent wants and expects a masculine little boy or a feminine little girl. No one expects, and certainly no one hopes for, an effeminate son or a masculine little girl. Our genderqueerness troubles them. Parents of kids like us sometimes do not know how to love us.

And it's not just when we come out or transition. I think we smell differently to our parents practically from the day we're born. They know something about us is different, and it terrifies and, alas, sometimes repels them. Some reject what they cannot understand or accept.

As a parent I try to give my daughter that glimpse of the infinite every day. Whatever trials await her in adulthood, when she moves forever beyond my grasp or the arc of my protection I want her to look back and know without a shred of a doubt that she was totally and perfectly loved.

I fail at that perfection every day. I'm in a bad mood. I'm too close, or I'm too far. I get caught up in work, and I lose one of these last few precious remaining days when we can still play unselfconsciously together, before she enters the cauldron of her teenage years.

I console myself that, at least, most of my failures are small ones. I hope I get the big things right. I do not dream of the dead, and certainly not of my family. But last night my mother came to me in the seconds before my alarm. She was so real, I actually reminded myself that I was dreaming. I said, *I feel great tenderness towards you, and great affection.* She smiled and we hugged. And then she turned away.

Children grow up loving their parents. If they are not loved in return, they may hate them. Sometimes, if they are very lucky, they are able to forgive them.

April, 2017

I Was Recently Informed I Am NOT a Transsexual

I was giving my Gender 101 presentation to an important corporate client in the Bay Area recently, when I got to the Terms & Definitions. It was then I learned I am no longer a transsexual. I tried to define the difference between "transgender" and "transsexual" but was stopped by three young persons—two of whom identified themselves as nonbinary—who took strong exception to the word *transsexual*.

"We don't use that anymore," they said. This was backed up by a young cisgender man, a UCLA Queer Studies major, who declared that the term was objectionable because it "medicalizes" transpeople, and inappropriately ties recognition of someone's genital status—which is private—to their gender identity. So it was not only archaic, but offensive.

I'd long known I was offensive—often intentionally so, more often unconsciously. But it was the first time I learned I was also archaic. You could hear the room stirring, and everyone's attention swiveling towards me, smiles gone, tense with that awful feeling when conflict breaks out over the politically incorrect.

"Politically incorrect" used to mean something like, *"We now have a better and more sensitive way to say that,"* which is actually a very helpful and useful correction to unconsciously offensive modes of communication that are deeply embedded in our language. And there are many. Yet it often comes with a hint of moral superiority, which has since grown to be as important as the subject that occasions it.

Now "politically incorrect" is closer to saying something like, *"I denounce you for having said something which we no longer say in polite company. You are therefore a bad person and should be publicly shamed, not to mention silenced."*

Sometimes this is right on target (Mr. President, call your answering service). However, just as often, this kind of brickbat is aimed at friend and ally who are simply one step behind the discourse...

...which of course is constantly changing, so that you often don't realize you've transgressed until you do it. This generates ever new opportunities to be pronounced "politically incorrect." It happens in every language. Even among the deaf—as the *New York Times* has noted—signs evolve in order to respond to new awareness and new sensibilities.

So no, we don't say *"gay and lesbian"* anymore, we say *"lesbian and gay."* Nor do we say *"lesbian, gay, and bisexual."* What we now say is *"lesbian, gay, bisexual, and transgender."* But, actually, it's lesbian, gay, bisexual, and... oh, screw it.

I don't mind having my language corrected. God

knows sometimes it is in need of correcting. Like everyone, I get things wrong, and I sometimes find myself on the wrong side of the gender discourse. But who has the right to certain terms is not just about PC, but also deeply intertwined with body and identity. It's not just *what* is said, but *who* does the saying.

It dawned on me that these three individuals probably read me as another privileged straight white cisgender male who was offensively referring to someone's genital status. My co-facilitator took me aside and told me that our training was toast. There was enough bad blood and moral indignation hovering over the meeting to make it impossible for us to continue. But I wasn't so sure. I always assume my transgender-ness is apparent, though in this room I was obviously wrong. I needed to come out.

So I explained that... ahem... I started my own transition in 1976, and that *"transsexual"* was indeed the term-of-art. We used it. Those around us used it. The book many of us read was entitled *"The Transsexual Phenomenon."* I co-founded a nationwide protest group called *"The Transexual Menace"* (No mistake, one S by intention). And, oh yes, I had my own surgery before any of you were born.

The atmosphere in the room became instantly warmer. The straight white oppressive male had morphed into... an oppressed, marginalized transgender person. So who is politically incorrect now? The sex change was on the other foot.

We are at an interesting place in queer discourse when it comes to the politics of trans self-description. There are now rules for what we can call ourselves. I love that transpeople are now considered legit enough that we can finally enjoy the luxury of telling people how we'd like to be referred to.

We used to be a despised class—a trash-bin of bodies and identities left behind when gay rights decided to mainstream itself by throwing its genderqueers under the bus (with some of us still having treadmarks to show for it).

At the time, we were happy just to be mentioned, regardless of what we were called. We were the identity that didn't speak its name. Now we can't get other folks to shut up about us. There's a news story about trans every week in most major newspapers, and on most high-traffic websites. My ten-year-old daughter calls me over to watch whenever she comes across another YouTube video featuring a trans character. We are everywhere.

So in addition to no longer being a transsexual, I also realized I am no longer a *trannie*. Yet, in spite of being regularly corrected when I use the term, I have a stubborn affection for it; same as *queer*, another word I like—one which LGBTQ people have fought hard for and successfully reclaimed from the pejorative it was.

I accept that "*trannie*" is diminishing and offensive. But I think it important to remind people (and maybe ourselves as well) that we have been diminished and considered offensive. I think it is important to always bear in mind where we've come from, and not just acknowledge the better and more-PC place we're hoping to go to.

Et Tu, Wachowskis?

The remarkable Netflix series, *Sense8*, by the Wachowski sisters, is now in its second season. It is an elaborate envisioning of another race of humanoids, *homo sensorium*, who communicate telepathically and live among us. These come in "clusters" that are scattered around the world, and from its opening credits *Sense8* is careful to present the viewer with the enormously diverse quilt that is humanity itself.

The opening credits roll over a stunning montage of multi-colored crowds, couples, celebrations and rituals from around the globe (yes, the show has a break-the-piggybank travel budget).

The cluster of eight we follow is diversity itself: a Kenyan, a German, an Indian, an Icelander, a Brazilian gay man, and a Bay Area transgender woman, among others. In nearly every episode, a cluster character denounces humanity's unfortunate propensity to fear and oppress those we see as different, as "the Other."

And yet, and yet...

Not a single genderqueer anywhere. Not in this cluster. Not in the others. Not in any character they interact with. Even the crazy underground computer hacker named "Bug" is, like everyone else, quite gender normative.

Apparently gender difference is "the Other" that must not speak its name.

And this is from a team where not one but BOTH siblings have bravely and publicly transitioned to be transwomen.

Moreover, all of this occurs in science fiction, a medium invented to let creative imaginations run wild with possibility. Apparently queerness is not among the possible. And, *Sense8* is hardly alone.

In the latest installment in the (now interminable) X-Men series (*Logan*), everyone is comfortingly gender normative. In the latest installment in the (now interminable) Aliens series (*Covenant*), everyone is comfortably gender normative. And in the latest installment of the (now interminable) Star Wars series (*The Force Awakens*) everyone is comfortingly gender normative (even Jabba the Hutt was not only male, but totally hetero—across species!).

Let this sink in—because it shows exactly what genderqueers are up against.

Mutants cannot be us. Even droids like C3PO cannot be us. Even dark, scaly alien creatures that are perfect killing machines, that drip acid for blood, come with nasty double-mouths, that burst from the human chest during birth, and drip gobs of gooey saliva before puncturing our skulls are nicely, neatly divided up into boys and girls (the girls lay the eggs, of course).

In short, even our best creative minds are simply unable to imagine, under any circumstances, on any world, in any galaxy, in any alien form, a character who is nonbinary and/or profoundly gender nonconforming (no, please do NOT feed me Whoopi Goldberg as Guinan on Star Trek).

This implicitly promotes binary male/female as some sort of unavoidable, universal, and implacable Natural Law, from which can be is no escape. As with The Borg (yes they were binary, too), "Resistance Is Futile."

One of the few exceptions was Stargate's lovely and genderqueer actor Jaye Davidson. Alas, Jaye's genderqueerness was introduced as evidence of otherworldly evil—all the "normal" people were binary. Even in a totally different universe, at the other end of a Stargate, all the aliens turn out to be boys and girls just like us (the girls do the cooking, and offer themselves up to the boys, of course).

Perhaps for a truly genderqueer sci-fi character we must wait for Taylor on Showtime's series *Billions* to don a spacesuit and launch a hedge fund on Tatooine.

Sadly, it is to be expected that cisgender people cannot imagine us. But it is beyond sad that even when we are behind the camera *and* behind the typewriter, as with *Sense8*, *we* cannot imagine us either. And this blind-spot is especially disheartening in a show that so pointedly wears its inclusive politics on its sleeve.

One has to wonder if there's a coming split one day in the trans community between those of us who are trans- and gender-conforming and those who of us who are trans- and gender-nonconforming. Right now we're all at sea together, politically, and so we're more or less rowing in the same boat.

But that was once true of the gay community, too. Then they started mainstreaming, and the genderqueers and transpeople were pushed towards the back so that gender normative gays and lesbians could be out front.

Will the trans movement go the same way? Will we split into those who are normatively binary and those who are genderqueer? How can we stay together when some of them can't even imagine that some of us exist?

The famous tagline from the first Aliens movie was "*In space, no one can hear you scream.*" Today it should be updated to "*In space, no one can imagine queers.*"

May, 2017

"Manning Up" for the Feds, with Undocumented Genitals

The Associate Press finally updated its official Style Guide to include "they," although Paula Froke, lead editor for the Guide, noted acerbically that it should be used "sparingly,"saying that "it's usually possible" to write around it. And probably better to write around *us,* too.

We seem, at last, poised to enter the Age of Genderqueer. I would like to think of the A/P as needing to reverse that position in a few years, explaining that "he" and "she" are acceptable, but should be used "sparingly" and that it's usually possible to write around rigid binary pronouns.

It was about 20 years ago that I had my first run-in with the A/P Style editors. It was not a happy one. Just as now, transpeople were dying at a terrible rate. Brandon Teena was in the news, but he was the wrong face for the epidemic. Most of the victims were not white transmales living in farm country, but young, Black transwomen in urban cities.

The news coverage would mis-pronoun them, and

then misname them—insisting on using "he" and their male birth names, and even, in death, denying them the dignity and identification for which they had paid so dearly. It was horrible, and it misrepresented both the cause and the effect of their murder.

While it is far from true that every journalist, or even every news outlet, slavishly adheres to the A/P's style guide, they were the standard, and the place to start. At GenderPAC, we asked them for a meeting, and, with an assist from GLAAD, got it. This was actually a big deal, since this was a time when many national and regional gay groups were still proudly LGB-but-not-T.

What we got was two salty senior associate editors,used to adjudicating dangling participles and split infinitives, who were quietly amused to find themselves caught in the middle of an impassioned plea by a transgender political group. It was the highlight of their morning, and probably a story they shared around A/P water coolers for years.

But they made the change.

Of course, the very next murder a few weeks later was covered by some small-market newspaper whose writers completely ignored the Style Guide. But at least GPAC and GLAAD could protest and try to educate them. And eventually, coverage did change.

And now they've come around to "they." Even for transpeople, maybe the Age of Genderqueer is around the corner.

Which brings me to my recent filing with the federal government for Medicare. What dismayed and then angered me was that my card came back with big black bold letters marked MALE.

I haven't had to fight this particular fight for over a decade. I admit I was out of shape for it. The last time had been over a dozen years ago when I filed for my first passport. The State Department demanded proof of my surgery from the attending doctors (along with a lot of other really intrusive documentation).

It was humiliating, and I was enraged. Cisgender society just can't get over its fixation on genitals being equal to gender. They are always pointing at our genitals, commenting on or inquiring about our genital status, marking it down somewhere, using it as the excuse to oppress us or otherwise make sure we fit them into their insane and oppressive bathroom/driver's license/name-change/[fill in your own blank here] system, in the most degrading and stigmatizing manner possible.

But my surgery was in 1978. I was among that first big cohort after the pause that followed Christine Jorgenson's change. The doctors who did my treatment were old white guys at the Cleveland Clinic who are now all dead, or nearly so. And since the Clinic had long since closed its trans program, even getting medical records was difficult or impossible.

I faced the nightmare that wakes every transgender person with terror in the middle of the night. Yes, I suddenly had… *Undocumented Genitals.* After watching the nightmares the Republicans were visiting on innocent immigrants, I couldn't even imagine what the government would make of genitalia which had suddenly, and of their own accord…*gone rogue.*

After 40 years of living as female I could only guess what new indignities would be required to change my Medicare card. On the other hand, I didn't really want to get injured or sick and end up rooming with a guy, being addressed as "Mister" by doctors and nurses simply because that's what it said on my insurance card.

So I manned-up and called Social Security in DC, angry and sad and scared all at the same time, ready to fight to the death with whatever small-minded government bureaucrat stood between me and a Cisgender-Certified Groin.

I need not have worried. They were surprisingly polite, even solicitous, as were the two men at the local office they referred me to, who waved me to the head of the line, photocopied my driver's license and passport, and sent me on my way.

Two weeks later, a new card arrived. I didn't even need a panty-check. Think of that. The Social Security Administration was kinder to me than the Michigan Womyn's Music Festival. It fairly boggles the mind.

Maybe things *had* changed. A little. Maybe, as the Age of Genderqueer dawns, in just a few small ways, it does get better.

June, 2017

The Limits of Transgender?

I was talking with a woman who ran a large public company last year, and she was speaking about her son, who she explained was "nonbinary," and used "them/they" as pronouns. I asked how long he had been transgender, and she replied, "Oh he's totally straight and male with a girlfriend—he just hates male/female categories and says that gender binaries are so over."

My first response was, "Oh my god—we've gone too far!" But upon reflection, I realized a profound shift was taking place and a fundamental question was being posed.

As writer/activist Dana Beyer points out, "The *trans* in transsexual was about moving from one thing to another," and it was anchored in discomfort. One was going from male to female, or vice versa. This concept was more or less unconsciously grafted onto transgender.

When spiritual leader and activist Holly Boswell coined the term, it was to name an excluded middle in the spectrum: those who were neither transsexual nor crossdressers. But then it was gradually stretched to include all of us. Now it's a tiresome true-ism that "transgender" is a "broad umbrella term" for all those who are gender nonconforming, and a transgender political movement has grown up to represent this community's political interests.

Alas, this is not, and never was, true. While we're no longer supposed to use the term *transsexual*, what we have always had is a transsexual movement about one's right to change sexes.

On one hand, think of many of the issues that animate this movement: the right to use the correct bathroom, to serve openly in the military, to get name-change corrections, not to lose one's job when transitioning (or when outed!). These are all important and necessary things, but what they have in common is that they are all related to changing from one sex to another.

On the other hand, you cannot find any transgender or LGBT organization of any size that ever mentions stone butches, drag people, *or* crossdressers. And intersex and nonbinary folks seldom are mentioned. For political purposes, they hardly exist. So, not much room under that umbrella.

This is particularly unfortunate for crossdressers, who pretty much founded what grew into the modern transgender movement, who created many of its earliest institutions, and then had to stand by and see themselves left behind by it.

Now the transgender movement is being challenged by those who identify as nonbinary and genderqueer. But are these people transgender?

Transgender has also been about a conflict

between birth sex and social gender expression, e.g., "I don't look like what you'd expect of someone with my birth sex." The dissonance was located in cisgender society's mind, not the individual's.

For transsexuals, this was slightly different. They had a conflict between their birth sex and their inner sense of gender identity, e.g., "I feel like a man, but have a female birth-sex." The dissonance was located in the individual's mind, as well as in society's. This dissonance was,to use the old psychiatric term, a "dysphoria."

With nonbinary people, it is the identifying act of saying one is "nonbinary" or "gender-nonconforming" which is central to identity. Can one be transgender if one is not *really* transgender? Is the simple act of identification enough? If one is a gender-conforming "nonbinary," would that even "count" as being genderqueer?

Even if we do include such people within the transgender movement, how would you operationalize that politically? What bathrooms do we want nonbinary people to have the right to use? How do we want them to be integrated into the military? What category (or categories) do we want them to be able to have on their government-issued ID?

Many years ago some transsexuals started identifying as "intersex." In a way, this made sense, both because there is probably a cross-sex biological aspect to being transsexual, and because society still views us as some kind of third sex—a practice at least some intersex activists have embraced.

With the emergence of transpeople who identify as a nonbinary or a third sex, in many places their political interests will overlap and intersect. Perhaps that will include things like removing gender from government ID, etc.

This brings up another interesting question with which transpolitics will need to wrestle, eventually: Are nonbinary people cisgender? If I identify as NB and use the pronouns "they" and "them," but have no desire to change my body and generally wear clothes associated to my birth sex, and I cisgender? Can one be a cisgender transperson, or is that a conflict in terms?

Whatever the answer to that question, it's clear that what we are starting to see is a transformation in the discourse of transgender. What comes next, what takes its place, what is beyond those limits is going to very interesting. Are we unconsciously and finally treading towards the end of gender categories as we know them? It will be fun finding out.

July 2017

A Trans Bathroom in Cartagena

There is a gender neutral bathroom in the Cartagena airport. Really.

I write this with some amazement. Every summer my family tries to take a vacation to someplace outside the US. One of the most humiliating parts of this for me is bathroom access.

I usually wear several layers because airports, and often airplanes, can be over-air-conditioned. If I walked in, all six feet tall, with my short hair, lack of make-up, and rangy build, it's going to cause a hassle.

I could and have used the men's room on occasion, but it always feels wrong and humiliating.

It's not that I'm a virgin in that area; quite the contrary. I lived as a boy for the first 26 years of my life. But being surrounded by men doing intimate things, watching them pull out their junk at the urinals, just feels gross to me now. Come to think of it, it always did.

So I do the next best thing. I take off all my outwear and sling it over my rollerboard. I'm always wearing a T-shirt so women can see my (definite if diminutive size-B) chest. As I enter the Ladies Room, I run my hand fetchingly through my hair several times for anyone nearby.

This, along with the sight of my chest, seems to get me by. Women will stare, not to mention their boyfriends and husbands waiting just outside, but no one has stepped me or dimed me out to the cops. At least not yet.

I wash my hands as quickly as I can, or just skip it altogether. I get that anxious feeling until the moment I'm back safely in the hallway, and even then I sometimes check to see if there's anyone at my back.

It's not that I'm fooling anyone. I look about as much like a cisgender woman as I do a basset hound. It's just that I seem able to convince everyone that I probably don't belong in the Men's room either, and if I'm not female I'm at least femin-ish and harmless.

I hate it. I hate it every time. I especially hate it when my daughter needs me to take her, as happened in the airport, because she is now old enough to recognize this insipid dance I do to protect myself from cisgender prejudice, and watches, wordlessly discouraged, as I perform it.

Which brings us back to Cartagena. Cartagena, Colombia is a lovely Caribbean seaport town. What I mean to say is that it is not the center of the Politically Correct Universe. Nor is it stacked with slavering Social Justice Warriors.

Yet there is this bathroom. Like all the others, they dress it up a bit by also making it a baby-changing station, but let's face it: awareness of babies has been around a lot longer than awareness of transpeople, and they never bothered to create these third bathroom options until now. So clearly this is about transpeople, and the baby-changing thing is just along for the ride.

So as my daughter and I went into the room together, I began thinking about how incredible it felt for me not to have to do my little bathroom dance; for me to have a place where even I felt comfortable and safe from the stares or incipient hassles. Even in Cartagena.

I have thought of it a lot. At a small Cartagena boutique hotel in the Central Historical District, where we'd just stopped in for coffee, I had a similar experience: a metal bathroom symbol with a group of four people on it of unclear genders.

I don't think I'd ever seen this before—not even in the urban gay ghettos we tend to inhabit. Since it wasn't the standard boy/girl sign that every bathroom sports, the owner probably had to get it specially made.

It was just this random, small, wonderful statement about inclusion, and a desire to avoid someone gender-nonconforming feeling uncertain, unwelcome, or demeaned.

What to make of all this? I used to think that bathrooms were our Achilles Heel. It is diminishing and degrading to have to launch a political argument based on something as small, and personal, and kind of juvenile as the need to pee. We have so many more important and pressing issues. Who wants to make a big public deal about needing to pee-pee? I haven't done that since kindergarten.

Okay, tenth grade. But still…you get my drift.

But I'm beginning to rethink that. This very prosaic-ness may actually be a strength.

For one thing, the urgent need for a restroom is also something everyone can relate to—trans and cisgender alike, and our pressing need to urinate has become a vivid illustration of the full breadth of unseen and unrecognized challenges that those of us who are gender-different face every day. And unlike hormones or surgery, it has deeply affected trans-kids as well. Again, unlike hormones, surgery, or even employment discrimination, it affects you nearly any day—every time you leave your own home.

This is a small act that nearly every business or institution, from a huge Fortune 100 to a corner bodega, can think about and act on, because bathrooms are everywhere.

And if my Cartagena experience is any evidence, this awareness is now going viral, and global, and very quickly indeed. This would have been unthinkable just ten years ago.

So maybe it's a small change, but small changes can also be very profound—and profoundly encouraging, especially if you and your daughter need to use El Cuarto de las Mujeres in the Cartagena city airport.

July, 2017

Transphobia is No Longer a Slam-dunk

On Wednesday, July 26th, President Trump tweeted that transpeople will no longer be allowed to serve in the military. Predictably , all hell broke loose. People were justifiably outraged. But my immediate reaction was—he's overreached.

Let history also record that on Thursday, July 14th 2017, Rep. Vicky Hartzler (R-Mo.) introduced an amendment to the annual defense authorization bill that would put an end to the Pentagon's Obama-era policy of providing gender reassignment surgery for transgender service members, and it was passed overwhelmingly by the Republican-controlled House.

Actually, no.

It was defeated. No, that is not a typo. And with five votes to spare: 214 to 209.

The House, in which the Republicans outnumber Democrats by 239 to 190, could not muster the votes. 24 Republicans crossed the aisle to vote with a solid block of all 190 Democrats.

Denying free government funding for trannies to get sex change surgery? Folks, this is the closest thing to a slam dunk that Republicans have, and it failed. It failed.

I'm sure Vicky and her Freedom Caucus buddies (three more from Missouri alone) must be beside themselves.

This is a House that has been working to defund Planned Parenthood. It has successfully gone after everyone from Muslims to Mexicans on immigration. It has passed a law that the Congressional Budget Office (CBO) estimates would take health care away from 22 million Americans, and use that money to give modest tax cuts to the ultra-rich.

It has even supported the NRA, including the NRA's new proposal to back the right of the unborn to carry concealed weapons, presumably because new NRA studies have found that obstetricians are much less likely to perform abortions if they suspect the fetus might be able to bust a cap in their ass.

Okay, I made that last one up. But still, Vicky and the Caucus have been in the forefront of all of these fights.

And yet this Congress, surely the most conservative in living memory, cannot muster the votes to deny free sex change operations to trannies. Well I ask you: what is the world coming to?

This is actually a watershed.

First, it's amazing that all 190 Democrats stayed together and voted against this. Not one wavering Blue Dog Democrat, not even the dozen imperiled Democrats from districts the Trump Monster won were willing to vote against us. So Democrats have pretty much internalized transgender rights as a core part of the human rights package (never thought I'd say this, but Atta-boy, HRC).

But what to make of the two dozen Republicans?

First, you have to suspect that Speaker of the House, Paul Ryan (R-WI) and Majority Leader Kevin McCarthy (R-CA) did not have their hearts in this one, and declined to "whip votes" for it. Republicans in the House have tended to vote in lock-step on nearly everything. It's that kind of institution, that kind of party, and that kind of political moment.

Also this is a remarkable transformation in a country where trans service members only gained the right to serve openly in June, 2016, barely one year ago. So it's only been one year since trans service members can access "medically necessary" treatment.

Clearly we still have a way to go, since Secretary of Defense Jim Mattis has put a six-month's hold on the right of openly transgender recruits to be inducted into the military.

But second, you have to suspect the White House didn't have all that much stomach for this fight either, since they were pretty mum in response to the amendment's failure. Could we be on the precipice of trans medical care finally be accepted as (dare I say it) uncontroversial?

Part of this is undoubtedly the risks service members take. We've already had the first out lesbian killed in combat: Air Force Major Adrianna Vorderbruggen, who died along with six others a suicide bombing in Afghanistan in December, 2015.

Regrettably, sooner or later we will have a transgender service member KIA as well. It's hard to tell someone who is serving in your military, who is risking capture, death, or dismemberment to protect your freedoms, that you're going to take away and restrict their right to medical care.

And this will be true of other human rights too. As there are more out transgender service members, Republicans are going to find it harder and harder to attack them, and therefore us. They will not be an easy target for conservative attacks, and we will be less and less a political "slam dunk.". Because all of them are making us all proud.

Oh, and the reaction to Trump's new ban on trans in the military?

Republicans look to Senator John McCain on issues involving the military and defense. Just seven years ago, McCain was a firm "No" on repealing "Don't Ask Don't Tell," which would only have allowed gay Americans to serve openly.

But McCain immediately tweeted back at Trump that no American should be denied the opportunity to serve their country, regardless of their gender identity.

Then Senator Richard Shelby, a Republican from Alabama (I am not making this up) made pretty much the same argument only shortly afterwards.

And it was deeply disorienting for me to discover that the poster-child on the front page of the Washington Post for Republican push-back to trannies in the military was (wait for it…) Utah Senator Oren Hatch, who basically responded (I'm paraphrasing), "Well, um, they're just born this way, and so what the heck."

When Orrin and the Mormon Church are in our corner, we've probably gone too far. Even the head of the Joint Chiefs of Staff, the highest ranking military officer in the country, responded with pushback, stating publicly that nothing would be done without a lot of clarification, and that the whole thing was going through regular channels. Until then, the General declared, "we will continue to treat all of our personnel with respect." The heads of every branch of the armed services followed suit, with the head of the Coast Guard even vowing to protect his trans servicemembers (in effect promising to disobey his Commander in Chief).

And that's what a sea change looks like.

No, De-Transitioning Is Not "A Thing"

I recently refused to be interviewed for an upcoming article for very prestigious magazine which would certainly have been great exposure. The author (I won't name her, but you can find her amazing interview with Janet Mock if you surf a bit) was very sensitive to the community, and, while she never self-identified as such, I believe she may quite possibly be genderqueer herself.

But the request was to be interviewed for an article on de-transitioning transsexuals, specifically very butch lesbians, who are so victimized by this society's genderphobia that they decide to become transmen, or believe they actually are transmen. When this doesn't work out, they must de-transition.

The media, naturally, has picked up on this. And it's about to become a new front in the Trannie Wars. Having hated and mocked transpeople, we have become the media's darlings.

But the media thrives on drama, not neat endings, and no drama works without plot shifts. This is why whatever the media builds up it also tears down. I fear they're about to do this to us.

Whenever I was interviewed back in the 1980s I would always be asked about this one, famous, de-transitioned individual. He had started out as male, decided he was transsexual (using politically incorrect word here intentionally), stopped well short of surgery, and then had gone back to living as male.

I wish him no ill, and hope he has found peace. But then he went on one national talk show after another, telling his story, and showing how we poor trannies really couldn't be trusted to know our own minds, saying that we often mistook our own gender, and in general should be kept away from sharp implements which might hurt us, particularly surgical scalpels and the doctors wielding them.

While he had every right to tell his story, it—and he—were used all over to undercut us, and once again delegitimize transgender experience. This cisgender urge to delegitimize us, to push us back towards our birth sex, is always lurking nearby. And it is terribly hard to undo.

It seems strange now, but in the 1980s trans surgery was pioneered and instituted by large teaching hospitals who led the way, beginning with Baltimore Johns Hopkins.

But then one man, Paul McHugh, latched onto a biased study he helped commission that was designed to show that transsexuality (still using politically incorrect term here) was a mental problem.

Then, using this weaponized study, he wielded his enormous power as Chief of Psychiatry to kill the transgender program at Hopkins, and soon every other major hospital followed suit. To this day, he still says, "I'm not against transgender people, [but] anxious they get the help they need."—meaning not surgery, but the psychiatric help that, entirely coincidentally, his department could render. With friends like these, you don't need enemies.

McHugh is still authoring anti-transgender pieces cited by the radical right to attack us. As the Washington Post notes, it took 38 years—nearly four decades—for Johns Hopkins to finally repudiate McHugh and return to the field. Four decades. And then only after faculty at Hopkin's own Bloomberg School of Public Health finally and publicly denounced his policies.

And then there's Ken Zucker, founder of the Toronto-based Center for Addiction and Mental Health (CAMH), that has "treated" 500 pre-adolescent gender-variant children—essentially non-complaining "patients"—forcibly submitted by their parents to his care. This is "reparative therapy" for transchildren when diagnosing them with an infant version Gender Identity Disorder.

CAMH was only closed, and Zucker stopped from harming another defenseless transchildren in 2015, when an internal audit challenged his work. But he had been doing this since the 1970s. So again, four to five decades passed before his terrible work could be stopped.

So no, I won't be quoted in an article, however well-intended, on de-transitioning. You want to quote me in an article on the horrors of genderphobia, I'm all in. But not one that reignites or fuels in any way the wars over our legitimacy. I hope not to step ever again into that poisoned pond.

There's a reason those "de-transitioned transsexuals" that the media trots out are almost never ever those who have had surgery. I have a theory as to why that is. It involves a pretty embarrassing story.

When I was going for my surgery, I was one of the first lesbian transwomen my team had seen. Almost all the ones they had treated were all about boys and the disco stick. I was not. I insisted that they alter their current surgical treatment and create a functioning clitoris. They found that remarkable. I found any alternative simply ridiculous, almost, in my mind at least, maiming.

So to make sure I "really" wanted surgery, they made me wait an extra year. It literally almost killed me. I had the car, I had the hose, and God knows I had the desire.

When the year was finally up, they went to wheel me in, and I still almost jumped off the surgical gurney. Even after all that. It was that scary.

So don't tell me about de-transitioning transsexuals. Not everyone who de-transitions was ever really transsexual, or even trangender. It's a damned hard life sometimes. Write your piece without me, and leave the rest of us in peace.

September, 2017

On Missing Leslie Feinberg

It was under a huge, wet blue tarp at Camp Trans outside the Michigan Womyn's Music Festival that I first saw Leslie Feinberg hold an audience spellbound. That speech was to be our main presentation for the day, but all morning it had been raining intermittently, so we at first thought that would force us to cancel the event.

But Camp organizer Janice Walworth had thought ahead, unveiling an enormous blue plastic tarp and the poles with which to string it up. Even with the tent set up, many of us doubted that festival attendees would walk the now-muddy mile or so road out of the Michigan Womyn's Music Festival in the rain to attend.

But come they did, in twos and threes, silently assembling under the tarp as the rain slowly cleared. By kick-off time, 200 women sat quietly on the ground, waiting for Leslie. She did not disappoint them.

I saw Leslie do it again the night before the vigil outside the murder trial for Brandon Teena's killers in Fall City, NE. Forty of us had come, and transactivist Davina Gabrielle had organized a town hall speak-out in nearby Kansas City. Leslie held the entire room enthralled with an impassioned speech about violence

116

against transgender people, and about Brandon's recent death.

This was all very different from when I first moved to New York City. Then, Leslie was mainly known for her relationship with Amber Hollibaugh, who was already recognized as a brilliant theorist and passionate activist.

In this time before "transgender," everyone seemed to be either male-to-female or female-to-male. Leslie was complex, in gender and in politics. And no one could quite figure out what Leslie was doing.

To begin with, Leslie identified as female-bodied, butch, lesbian, *and* transgender. For pronouns, it was all about context: "she/her" in non-transgender settings but also "he/him" to honor Leslie's gender expression in other situations. Plus the gender-neutral "ze/hir" were always welcome.

Politically, Leslie described herself as "an anti-racist, white, working-class, secular Jewish, transgender, lesbian, female, revolutionary communist." This was a lot. Perhaps too much for any of us to digest in our binary male/female, transsexual-oriented frameworks. Whatever else, Leslie floated on the periphery just outside of everyone's awareness, beyond our binary categories.

In the end it was our categories that changed, not Leslie.

Stone Butch Blues came out. And it seemed to mine a whole butch/fem subculture of lesbian life which writers and activists like Amber and Joan Nestle had also been working to resuscitate for years, but which had fallen out of favor as too binary and "politically incorrect."

Ironically, Leslie, who had little use for binary definitions personally, gave this butch/fem identity a power and presence and immediacy it had never enjoyed before. But even more, Leslie used butch/fem as a foundation to speak directly to the experience of tens of thousands of enraptured readers well beyond the subculture, who also knew the pain, ridicule, rejection, and danger of being in some way genderqueer. The book and Leslie's identity caught something in the zeitgeist. Leslie became not just an instant celebrity, but zir *Stone Butch Blues* provided enormous visibility to the growing movement for transgender rights.

It was about this time that my own first book, *Read My Lips*, came out. It was a difficult, personal, angry, sometimes theoretical book, over which I had labored for years. And I could only watch *Blues'* book sales with envy, sometimes wishing I had written fiction instead, but wondering if I could ever be as good at it.

Leslie brought to these public appearances an amazing personal presence. Part of this was a ruggedly handsome profile that was made to be struck on coins or modeled in bronze. Then there was the distinct, raspy voice, that always conveyed a passion for tough causes. And then this tremendous awareness of power and privilege which was likely informed by her deep communist-socialist beliefs.

I remember speaking at a college town once, at a time when I was everyone's second speaker-of-choice. The students would pick me up at whatever airport and proudly inform me that, "We had Kate Bornstein last year," or, "Leslie keynoted our last Pride Parade." I knew this was offered to please me, though I gritted my teeth in an agreeable smile.

I was often tired and worn out from the flight, and the cars sent to pick me up were always small subcompacts with three or four students on the greeting committee crammed in along with my six-foot frame. I would always take the front passenger seat to have a little bit of legroom, being careful to avoid the inevitable hamburger wrappers, French fry containers, and crumpled term papers on the floor.

Then someone happened to mention that Leslie, who had probably taken the same flights from NYC, and was no doubt just as tired, always insisted on sitting in the back seat, to honor the work of the local activists. I could only wince.

I think that was one of the main reasons Leslie stopped talking to me. I was too *bourgeois,* and when I launched GenderPAC, I effectively joined the traditional DC beltway political establishment which I suspect Leslie disdained, and which was, in any case, oppressive and quite unrepresentative.

Moreover, I could not see any way to map a transgender politics onto the economics of class struggle, to which Leslie had devoted their life.

The last time I saw Leslie speak was to an entire congregation of people who had turned out for a Boston memorial vigil for Chanelle Pickett, organized by transactivist Nancy Nangeroni.

In the years of sad events for dead transgender people I have attended, this was easily the saddest. Chanelle's identical twin sister, Gabrielle, who was also trans, spoke in simple grief and dignity to the crowded church about her murdered twin. To this day, even with an identical twin as my wife, I simply cannot imagine. We could not know she herself would be killed in NYC under similar circumstances only a few years later. As I said, it is the saddest of many sad stories.

Leslie was brilliant that day. When it came time to ask for donations, Leslie said something to the effect of, "If I'm not here with you to carry on the struggle...."

I thought to myself that that was probably effective fundraising, but it seemed a bit dramatic, a bit of *workin' the crowd*. I had no way of knowing that Leslie was already struggling with serious health complications, including those from Lyme Disease. There are some people—Kate, of course, is another—without whom you cannot imagine the trans movement. They inhabit a unique space that was not there before, but which you cannot imagine being without, and which has come to feel entirely necessary and totally irreplaceable. Leslie was like that. The last time I saw Leslie was at an underground gym in Chelsea on 18th Street and Sixth Avenue called Better Bodies. Leslie still looked healthy and strong. We were both working out. I nodded, but Leslie looked through me and continued on to the weight rack.

September, 2017

The Last Transgender Teen Suicide

Yet another heartbreaking newsstory on the wire services last week:

"[Kings Mills OH - 11 Jun

17-year-old LeaAnne Acorn posted a suicide note to her Tumblr account explaining that she had felt like a girl since she was four, that her parents had completely rejected her on religious grounds and instead forced her into treatment with a local psychiatrist, and that she was ending her life. At about 2:15 a.m., LeeAnne walked out on Interstate 71 in front of an oncoming tractor-trailer, and was killed immediately.

In her Tumblr note LeeAnne explained, "After 10 years of confusion I finally understood who I was. I immediately told my mom, and she reacted extremely negatively, telling me that it was a phase, that I would never truly be a girl, that God doesn't make mistakes, that I am wrong. If you are reading this, parents, please don't tell this to your kids. Even if you are Christian or are against transgender people, don't ever say that to someone, especially your kid. That won't do anything but make them hate their selves. That's exactly what it did to me."

Usually no one is punished for these suicides. But now the American Psychiatric Association's new diagnostic manual, the DSM-5, addresses transsexuality as a physical disorder, not a mental one. Even better, the major medical groups led by the American Academy of Pediatrics (AAP) and the American Medical Association (AMA) finally recommend hormone blockers and similar treatment for trans-kids that fit the emerging "consistent, persistent, and insistent" protocol: that is that the patients are consistent in their gender identification, they persist in it over time, and they insist that something be done about it.

In other words, you can no longer torment trans-kids by denying their gender, refusing to acknowledge their pain, ignoring their physical needs, and instead forcing them into "reparative" psychiatric treatment and medication, as LeeAnne's parents did.

So it was a relief to finally see this follow-up hit the wires:

[Cincinnati OH - 14 Jun]

The parents of 17-year-old transgender teen LeaAnne Acorn, who committed suicide after they denied her access to medical treatment on religious grounds, were taken into custody early this morning by the Kings Mills Sheriff's Department. Both are being charged with one count each of involuntary manslaughter, child neglect, and child endangerment. They are being held pending bail. Their attorney refused to comment on the case.

Finally trans-kids have some rights.

Except that, of course, they don't. Because this "Acorn" story didn't happen that way. It's the way it should have happened, but it didn't.

In fact, it's really based on the sad story of Leelah Alcorn.. Leelah killed herself December 28, 2014 and her parents faced no legal consequences whatsoever for their actions which—according to Leelah's own words—led to their daughter's death. But there is precedence for changing that.

For instance, this past February, two Pennsylvania parents who belonged to a fringe religious sect were charged with involuntary manslaughter and child endangerment after declining to seek medical care for their two-year-old's entirely treatable pneumonia—instead insisting on prayer, and awaiting "God's will," while she slowly succumbed.

This is not far from Leelah's situation. And these laws (albeit with religious exceptions often carved out) are now common and nearly universal in the 50 states.

They establish that parents are responsible when they do nothing in the face of a child's illness. So no, there aren't strongly recommended treatment protocols for trans-kids... yet. But there will be; they are coming.

Join me for a moment in the year 2030. AAP and AMA have fully recognized standard treatment protocols for trans-kids, including acknowledgement of their correct gender, hormone blockers at first, and then full hormone treatment in puberty for those who meet the "consistent, persistent, and insistent" standard.

And these standards are now widely followed. Denying medical treatment for a child suffering with a diagnosis of Gender Dysphoria is no different from denying medical treatment for a child suffering with a diagnosis of Bacterial Pneumonia.

What will happen to parents like Leelah's then? Will purposefully withholding and denying treatment that results in yet another transgender teen suicide be grounds for law enforcement to act, and for bringing charges of involuntary manslaughter or child endangerment?

You bet it will. It will probably be implemented first in one of the Scandinavian countries, which are always well ahead of us on nearly everything progressive.

But eventually it will come here as well. And there will finally be *legal* consequences for denying trans-kids the care their bodies cry out for.

Even today, many progressive parents are already following these emerging standards. Some—perhaps without realizing it—are also saving their daughters' and sons' lives in the process.

These parents are on the leading edge of what will one day be standard everywhere. And that day can't come soon enough. Because there are still so many Leelah's out there—lonely, suicidal, desperate for treatment and even more desperate for simple recognition—children whose immense suffering and untimely deaths could so easily be averted, if only we gave transkids the most basic medical rights when it comes to their bodies and genders.

Part II

From *Read My Lips: Sexual Subversion and the End of Gender*

Foreword

First, since I wear several hats (not to mention any number of ill-fitting dresses), let me state from the outset that I do not write in any official capacity nor represent anyone but myself. In any under-represented community, there is always the danger that the few voices lucky enough to be heard end up being cast as representatives. The same dangers apply here. Few trans-identified folk will agree with everything (or perhaps even a majority) of this book.

In fact, under the broad label "transpeople" there is an extraordinarily rich and vibrant diversity which continues to grow and expand. Our own margins, in terms of race, ethnicity, class, and even divergent sub-identities, are still silent and waiting to be heard from. Here's hoping it happens sooner than later.

In any case, the idea of being a spokestrans has always seemed absurd to me. If three transpeople go into a room together they emerge with five opinions among them. We are that opinionated and stubborn; we have to be to survive.

So when you read some particularly bizarre sally with which you truly disagree, rest assured that I am not a community spokestrans, nor do we all sit around discussing gender theory and politics every night. All the opinions here are my own. Now that I think of it, the ones you like are mine; those you don't, I'll let you think were suggested by my editor or publisher— probably both.

From C to Shining C

While we're on language, I might as well address the dreaded C words, both of which you will find herein: cock and cunt. It's not that I get off on being smutty-mouthed (of course I do), but in my experience it's the way people talk. For those who find their C word distressing, I can only point out that I came of age in a lesbian community in which we reclaimed and employed it with a certain insubordinate and affectionate abandon. I use it in the same spirit here.

On Constituencies: Transgender v. Transsexual v. Trans

Who knows what to call transpeople these days? The dominant discourse in the transcommunity is at best a moving target. Transgender began its life as a name for those folks who identified neither as crossdressers nor as transsexuals—primarily people who changed their gender but not their genitals. An example of this is a man who goes on estrogen, possibly lives full-time as a woman, but does not have or want gender recognition surgery.

The term gradually mutated to include any genderqueers who didn't actually change their genitals: crossdressers, transgenders, stone butches, intersex, and drag people. Finally, tossing in the towel on the noun list approach, people began using it to refer to transsexuals as well, which was fine with some transsexuals, but made others feel they were being erased.

I personally believe that transgender has succeeded where transsexual failed because people are more comfortable saying it out loud because the latter term—if you hold the word up in the mirror and read it backwards—has the word "SEX" cleverly imbedded in it.

In addition, many folks are moving away from "transssexual," because it sustains the long-standing cisgender imperative to *genitalize* gender, reducing it and us to the status of our gentials, which is both intrusive and disparaging. Notwithstanding that, I have used the term to refer specifically to that sub-group of transpeople who want to or have changed sexes. And I continue to use it to refer to my own experiences in coming out, since we were, quite specifically perceived as "transsexuals."

To pick just one example, there were many kinds of trans and very genderqueer women at the Michigan Womyn's Music Festival—it was practicaly an annual gala for them—but only those of us who self-identified, or whom security suspected as being "transsexual," were evicted. While I support the move to *de-genitalize* gender, it's important to recognize that terms like "transsexual" don't just medicalize gender, but can also denote a specific *poliitcal* experience of it.

"Transgender" was first used by activist and trans-spiritual leader Holly Boswell to describe those who were neither transsexuals nor crossdressers. Soon after, it evolved into what is inevitably described as a "broad umbrella term," defined by its inclusions rather than its boundaries, one in which anyone who is (in Kate Bornstein's felicitous phrase) "transgressively gendered" was welcome.

Alas, the term is increasingly hardening into an identity to be defended from intruders rather than a welcoming descriptor open to all who want it.

For instance, I recently had a butch lesbian tell me she didn't want to "co-opt my voice," and so only identified herself as "small-t transgender." This was from a woman wearing slacks, flat shoes, a vest, and coat and tie. She was more transgender than I was.

I've also been asked repeatedly if I wasn't angry that so-and-so was publicly identifying as transgender because she wasn't "really" a transsexual, being "only" a drag person, or an intersex person, or a crossdresser, or a...[fill in offensive and appropriating identity here].

The result of all this is that I find myself increasingly invited to erect a hierarchy of legitimacy for trans, complete with walls and boundaries for me to defend—a project for which I not only have no interest but to which I'm quite actively opposed.

I am much more interested in challenging a gender system that compels each body (not just the trans ones) to answer to one of two binary identities, to express themselves as masculine or feminine, Woman or Man, and punishes those who don't fit, or those who seek to switch identities, or find themselves (like me) stranded somewhere in between.

I am much more interested in contesting the linguistic fiction that "real" gendered identities like transgender or transsexual, however broad and umbrella-like, actually existed prior to the oppressive systems that required us to announce ourselves through them. This seduction of language, constantly urging us to name the constituency we represent rather than the oppressions we contest, is a Faustian bargain through which the political legitimacy of identity politics is purchased.

I only regret that I have succumbed to that seduction myself too often. For this is not a book about identities, but about a common cultural machinery—one that repudiates, stigmatizes, and marginalizes many kinds of bodies.

This is not a machinery that harms only the gender-differerent and gender nonconforming. Indeed, three decades of research, practice, and theory have established beyond a doubt that rigid gender binaries are also harmful and even destructive to those bodies that *do* fit, and that do successfully internalize narrow masculine or feminine norms.

The gender system is why (for example) young Black men are perceievd as hyper-masculine, physically threatening, and 4.5 years older than they actually are. It is part of why young Latinas who buy into narrow womanhood ideals have higher rates of suicde than any other ethnic or racial group in America. It is part of why young men in low-income communities fear public vulnerabilty so much that they postpone medical care until their bodies are in crisis from treatable and even preventable illnesses. And it is why Black female students who fail to display submissive, white, middleclass forms of femininity in school are increasingly (in Kimberle' Crenshaw's phrase) "pushed out, overpoliced, and underprotected."

It is why privilege and opportunity in American continue to be deeply stratified by race, class, and gender.

131

A rigid binary gender system affects ALL of us, conforming and nonconforming, if in very different ways. It is an intentional and systemic oppression, and, as such, cannot be fought through personal action, but only through an organized and systemic response.

So while this book necessarily focuses on gender difference and queerness, it is not a book for *trans*persons, but rather for *all* persons interested in challenging and contesting that system. I hope you enjoy it.

Video Tape

(Read at a transsexual speak-out held at New York's Lesbian & Gay Community Center in 1993 in honor of the fortieth anniversary of Christine Jorgenson's sex-change surgery. She was the first American transwoman to become widely known in the U.S., making possible so much of what came after.)

Rewind

"It's beautiful," I exclaim. It is, in fact, a particularly fine watch my father has just bought for my seventh birthday, the jeweled face throwing back at me the summer's sunlight. "It's... it's..." I hesitate, searching for just the right word, "it's *divine*", I breathe happily. My father's face comes up sharply, his pupils narrowing. "Boys don't say divine." And he watches me, his head cocked slightly to one side. I open my mouth to question this unfathomable statement, as if certain dictionary words were colored blue for boys and pink for girls, but there is something hard in his voice and eyes and, suddenly, my pleasure evaporates and is replaced by fear. I know if I question him I'll probably get the palm of his hand. When a six-foot-two-and-a-half inch, 200 pound man hits you in the face with his open hand, it's like being hit in the head with a ham. And, so, mumbling something to my feet like, "Well, it is very nice," I make a small mental note to avoid this particular word in the future.

Fast Forward

The woman sitting across from me is so butch, she is often mistaken for a man. We have been discussing the pros and cons of her beginning testosterone treatments. But at the moment, she is lecturing me on being more feminine. "You sometimes—I don't want to hurt your feelings—but you sit crosslegged in meetings and sometimes it takes up some of the space of the woman next to you. As a woman, I just wouldn't do that. It's your male training, like the men on the subway who have to spread their legs and take up two seats. You don't understand how intimidating to women male behavior can be."

Quick Rewind

I have been invited as a guest panelist at the Lesbians Undoing Sexual Taboos (LUST) conference for women. I sit when I'm done speaking, sensing the pressure that has built up in the room. The women start applauding, and it just goes on and on and on. I sit. I can't even look at this stunning validation, this unbelievable, unsought welcome back into some kind of women's community after I left all that behind 12 years ago in Cleveland. Later, in response to an audience question, I remark how strange it is to be an honored guest at an event that probably would have tossed my ass out ten years ago. It's like riding the crest of a wave. What a strange thing—to be on the edge of a coming change, a change you have waited for, hungered and worked for, that suddenly begins to happen all around you.

Forward, Normal Speed

One of the exciting things to come out of the LUST conference is that a woman is planning a dinner and sex party for 100 women. Oh boy, does this sound hot or what? I've been waiting about a decade for something like this to happen. I find one of the fliers at the Center. As I quickly scan the brochure, I see on the bottom of the last page: *no men, no transvestites, and no transsexuals*. Riding the crest of a wave indeed. The board has just flipped and I have a mouthful of saltwater. For once, I've got to confront someone who is discriminating against me, if only to talk. I call, just asking for a dialogue, a chance to at least explore our differences. After a few minutes she tells me I'm simply a transvestite who has mutilated himself and hangs up.

Rewind

Eighth grade math class. I cannot hear what the teacher is saying. In fact, I don't care what she's saying. I am totally mesmerized by the sight of Dara Rosen's new young breast disappearing into the cup of her new bra, something I can just barely see as she sits across from me in her sleeveless dress. Worse, I am torn between wanting desperately to touch that soft breast and wanting desperately to have that soft breast.

Fast Forward

I am on the trading floor at Republic National Bank. It is the third day of my nine-month consulting contract. One of the block traders far down the floor is taking down everyone's name and phone extension and when he gets to me, he calls for me to spell out my name. I do, and he yells back, "Riki, that's cute. Where'd that come from?" "Well", I respond, "it used to be Richard." The heads of two distant block traders down the floor, intently tracking the DOW movement on their monitors, swivel sharply around as if on soundless ball bearings. They stare briefly at me before returning to the DOW. My boss, sitting next to me, who has come to Wall Street from a very gay 12-year career in musical theatre, chuckles softly without even looking up from his screen. He is having more fun with this than a pig in shit.

Forward, Normal Speed

My new boss, a 25-year-old NYU finance graduate, is staring intently at my chest. Actually, not my chest, but the area on my coat over my chest—just over my heart, on the left side. I've been a little intimidated here at J.P. Morgan. I've spent a year-and-a-half trying to get a consulting contract here and I'm finally in. I look down, knowing helplessly that I'm probably wearing some of my breakfast. Just what I need. But I am not. What I am wearing is my *Take a Transsexual to Lunch* button, which I wear everywhere *but* into work and which, this morning of all mornings, I have neglected to remove.

Rewind

My friend Deborah has offered to stay over with me, and since it's my first night back home from surgery, I gratefully accept. We lie quietly in bed together. She's holding me gently. "Can I feel?" she asks after a minute. "Yes, but I have a dilator in so you can't really go inside. She puts her hand between my legs anyway. "Can I move it?" she asks. "Sure, why not." I have no thought on this subject, just a kind of curiosity and a small, flaming desire to lose whatever kind of virginity this is, after losing so many others. She pushes gently, firmly, on the dilator as her body leans towards mine. For the first time in my 28 year-old life, I feel a woman moving inside me, in my vagina.

Fast Forward

I am at a private, very underground lesbian women's S/M night at "Paddles" here in New York, having been invited by Pat Califia who, by many accounts, began this movement. This is, at best, a completely super-marginalized minority within a minority, which New York's Finest can raid with complete impunity at any time they choose during the evening. A woman approaches me, dressed entirely in shining black leather from neck to toe, and holding a rather substantial riding crop. She flexes it as we talk. After a few minutes, she confides that she finds me very attractive, and wonders if I enjoy being whipped, because she would very much like to whip me. As we continue talking, and I mention I am transsexual, she freezes, stares intently, and looking a bit green around the gills excuses herself hurriedly to stalk across the room, where she and several of her cisgender, leather-clad, lesbian-feminist, sado-masochistic (I'm running out of hyphens here) friends can stand and giggle and point at someone as strange and unique as me.

Rewind

Dad is climbing through the fence, which is made of barbed wire strands, strung from fence posts all over this farm where we are hunting pheasant. It is freezing cold with a half foot of snow on the ground, but we are both bulkily dressed and shod against the weather and the wind that gathers speed, blowing across the open fields. To get through the fence, to separate and hold the rusted barbed wire, he has to hand me his big 12-gauge shotgun, which I hold along with my smaller, lighter 20-gauge. As he climbs through, I can see the only thing around us, the clubhouse, far over his shoulder in the lonely distance, a single black silhouette against the gathering sky. I tell myself I can do it. I can say I dropped it and it went off, and inside my head a little pounding begins and small quivers are starting to knot my stomach and shoulders. You wouldn't really, I say to myself, but already I can see the look of surprise, that final, complete grasp of fact, as the shotgun goes off, blowing a hole in that bastard that only a 12-gauge shotgun at very close range can make, a hole I could put my entire 13 year-old fist through, the sound echoing off the clubhouse and back at us, locked in that moment, gratefully and mercifully our last moment together. Me knowing I am free, finally, at last. They'll believe me if I cry, if I withdraw into myself. I know how to do months of silent, strained shock to hide from people. He has at least taught me that. And then I imagine the devastation to my mother and our lives, and the years of questions and forms and police and authorities and, while I am thinking of all this, he is through the fence and reaches for me to hand him his gun, no thought in his head but that I obey instantly, as usual, and, like a puff of air, the single moment of safety and freedom hits me and is gone.

Fast Forward

Jaye Davidson is going to pull the trigger. She is absolutely going to pop that cisgender, IRA bitch. I am watching *The Crying Game*, which every cisgender friend and acquaintance has told me I *must* see, and I'm remembering being in that final, pre-surgical meeting at the Cleveland Clinic. I am in tears surrounded by about eight doctors and a dozen perky young nurses, trying desperately to convince those sodden bastards that, yes, I am a transsexual and, yes, I want them to make sure I have a functioning clit when they're done carving up my groin because, yes, I do still get hot for women and I look forward to them going down on me. One doctor has asked me with barely suppressed disgust how I would feel if I couldn't have an orgasm (and how would you feel if your sorry-assed wienie-roasted limp-dick couldn't have an orgasm?) and another has pointed to his impossibly feminine, delicate WASP nurse, explaining patiently that I understand, of course, I won't come out looking like *her*, and I am thinking of all the women telling me that I can never be a real woman, presumably like them, and now phrases like *Women-born women only, Biological women only, Genetic women only*—or whatever exclusionary formula is in vogue with our very best lesbian thinkers this year— start tumbling over each other in my head like a bunch of manic puppies. I am thinking about all those feminine, self-satisfied, dismissive young Jewish girls I grew up with, went to synagogue with, hated and lusted for and lost sleep over, and I swear I am practically coming in my pants here in the theater seat as Jaye finally pulls the trigger on that cisgender bitch—not just once, the first shot echoing out and the surprise registering on those small, delicate, well-spaced features—just like I knew it would on my father's larger, heavier European ones. No, Jaye, my hero of the moment, my trans-savior, she pulls the trigger again and again and again and five, six, seven—how many shots are in an automatic?—until

139

that beautiful cisgender woman, the kind that, if we look like them, tell us how well we pass, she's down for the count and I'm telling myself frantically after four years of 12-Step programs that I'm not about violence and I've given up fighting anyone or anything. But the anger and tears rise in my throat with the bitterness of bile and stick there like some kind of demonic fishbone, and I know helplessly and a little guiltily that I'll rent this video, not for the directing which is nearly perfect, nor the storyline which is brilliant, but just to see Jaye pull that trigger in this scene again and again and again.

The problem with transsexual women is not that we are trapped in the wrong bodies. The truth is that that is a fairly trivial affair corrected with doctors and scalpels. The problem is that we are trapped in a society which alternates between hating and ignoring, or tolerating and exploiting us and our experience.

More importantly, we are trapped in the wrong minds. We have, too many of us for too long, been trapped in too much self-hatred: the hate reflected back at us by others who, unwilling to look at the complexity of our lives, dismiss our femaleness, our femininity, and our sense of gender and erotic choices as merely imitative or simply derivative. Wanting desperately to be accepted, and unable to take on the whole world alone, we have too often listened to these voices that were not our own, and forgotten what Alice Walker says when she declares:

...no person is your friend (or kin) who demands your

silence, or denies your right to grow and be perceived as

fully blossomed as you were intended. Or who belittles in
any fashion the gifts you labor so to bring into the world.

And our lesson is neither new nor unique. From Lyndal MacCowan:

"It means knowing I'm a freak. It means knowing that I am
not a woman. It means falling in love with girls and, at the
same time, despising their femininity, their obsession with
makeup and boys, their lack of strength and brains. It
means knowing that both the kind of woman I want and the
kind of woman I am don't exist, do not have names... If it
does not someday make me kill myself, it's something that
can get me killed."

Transsexuality? No, she's speaking about being a self-identified lesbian femme in the 70s and 80s. There are no new changes, just new faces.

In closing, let me tell you about one transsexual. After ten years of hiding and passing and sucking up to cisgender women, strung out and totally desperate, she started a transsexual group.

She started talking with them and hanging out with them and being seen with them, although at first she hated it, she started wearing buttons and coming out at every appropriate and inappropriate moment, just as if her life were as normal and natural as anyone else's. And she learned that, although she might hate herself, she could not hate the 50 or 100 other transsexuals she met, whose tears of frustration and rage she saw, whose every day one-day-at-a-time courage to survive she witnessed.

And she understood, at last, the redemptive power of community, and how it can only be stifled by self-hate and silence. Community, my friends and transsexual kin, is what we build here today, by coming together to claim our own, our history, and our own Christine, whom we honor here today. Christine, standing all alone in God's own light in a way none of us have had to since, made all of this and all of us possible.

Sex! Is a Verb

The Transexual [*sic*] Menace demonstrates at a reading Janice Raymond does at Judith's Room, the last of New York City's women's bookstores (and now defunct). She is what is called a TERF (Trans-Exclusionary Radical Feminist) and the author of a book which is easily the most hostile and transphobic ever. Raymond draws about two dozen people who are obviously bewildered to be in the midst of an equal number of genderqueers in black Menace T-shirts. By prior agreement with the owners, Raymond and I engage in a debate following her reading. I am taken aback as she immediately exclaims, "But why would you want to do that to your body?"

"Do what?" I ask.

"Well, have it cut into, change your sex."

"How do you know I've had surgery?"

"Well, I mean I assume...," she trails off, gesturing vaguely at my Menace T-shirt and looking baffled.

"But why would you care? At the risk of sounding heartless, Dr. Raymond, I don't give a damn what you do with your body."

Meet Me In the Dark, Under the Small Part Of That Curve, You Know,Where All the Hot, New Anomalies Hang Out

Is there one sex or two? Or, including the intersexed, how about three or four? The argument that intersex bodies are pathology doesn't help us much, because—assuming the bodies are perfectly functional—that's a value judgment masquerading as medical fact.

Saying the intersexed comprise just a "negligible" fraction of the population doesn't help us, either. It just takes us out of the land of Fact and Nature, plopping us squarely in the squishy realm of Probabilities and Chance. Deciphering this begins to look suspiciously more like cultural judgment than the cold eye of Impartial Science.

Attack of the Intersex People!

Who gets to say which bodies "count," and why? How small a number of a certain kind of body can there be and have it still be considered "negligible." Whose body is the standard for normal, against which all others are judged? How different can a body be before society decides to pathologize and "treat" it?

According to the Intersex Society of North America, about one in 2,000 births is intersex (also known as Disoders of Sexual Development or DSD). They estimate that five intersex infants are operated on in U.S. hospitals *each day*.

All of these operations, of course, are performed without the patients' consent. Intersex Genital

144

Mutilation (IGM) is imposed on these infants (many of whom have no health or clinical conditions) by a medical science simply to impose aesthetic norms on bodies that function perfectly well but are different.

Honest Officer, They Were Sexed Here When I Arrived

We're taught that while gender may come from Culture, sex comes from Nature. All bodies already have a sex *in* them. This sex is recognized and expressed by culture as gender through social practices like clothing, hairstyles, and whether one finds pastels simply *faaaaabulous*. In this narrative, sex is a natural property of bodies, while gender is just what culture makes of them. In Judith Butler's terms, "Sex is to Nature (raw) as Gender is to Culture (cooked)." The naturalness of sex grounds and legitimizes the cultural practices of gender. But what if this narrative is actually inverted?

The more we look, the less natural sex looks. Everywhere we turn, every aspect of sex seems to be saturated with cultural needs and priorities. Mother Nature has Mankind's fingerprints all over Her.

Maybe the formula is reversed. Gender is not what culture creates out of my body's sex; rather, sex is what culture makes when it genders my body. The cultural system of gender looks at my body, creates a narrative of binary difference, and says, "Honest, it was here when I arrived. It's all Mother Nature's doing." The story of a natural sex that justifies gender evaporates and we see sex standing revealed as an effect of gender, not its cause. Sex, the bodily feature most completely in-the-raw turns out to be thoroughly cooked, and our comforting distinction between sex and gender collapses. We are left staring once again at the Perpetual Motion Machine of gender as it spins endlessly on, creating difference at every turn.

Another Day in the Life of a Gendertrash Reject

What social systems make the recognition and lifelong attachment of a sex on my body possible? What cultural agencies push it along? Which institutions store and retrieve knowledge about my body, and at what points of contact with society is this information brought into play?

Let's take a walk around town. I've a busy day, so try to keep up. It's 1980 and I'm preparing for "sex-change" surgery, which is wonderful, but the timing is kind of a bummer since I have to register for graduate school at Cleveland State University. But I can handle it. I'm a genderqueer. I can handle anything.

My first stop is the Cleveland Clinic. My social worker makes notes as usual in my chart and I talk about how my life "as a woman" is going, whatever that means. I think it means how people are reacting to me and how I feel about it. But why should that count towards my surgery? I mean, it's going to be my body lying on the table, not theirs, and certainly not the Hospital's.

What is it like living "as a woman?" Well, between the stares in the bathroom with threats to call the cops, to the guys on the street who make sucking noises and comment on the teenage breasts growing on my 26 year-old body, it's no picnic. Everyone seems to be looking at my body and trying to do something about it. She scribbles away.

She asks me to sign these long, legal-looking documents. One says that I understand all the various procedures they're going to do; the other that I'm not married. Seems that after the operation I'll be considered legally female, so it would be illegal for me to be married. This takes them off the hook. Huh... so if I had a wife, our relationship would suddenly become a same-sex marriage. A loving union made in heaven becomes a crime with a flick of a blade. Oh, goody! She is not amused. I shut up and sign. She gives me a date for surgery.

From the medical bureaucracy to the civil bureaucracy. I go down to the County Recorder's office and don't even get to see a judge. Alas, I will miss the irony of a man who lives half his life running around publicly in a floor length black dress passing judgment on my gender. Instead, I get some bored clerk who looks like a third-year law student. He eyes me sourly from behind a battered desk, one of those broad, rough things that invites graffiti. I try to read the desktop art upside down while he examines my proof that I've publicized my legal change of name in the Cleveland Legal Register for the required 30 days.

He asks me how the sovereign state of Ohio can know I'm not doing this to defraud someone, because that kind of name change is strictly illegal. *I mean, look at me, asshole. I'm a guy in a dress who gets hassled in the restroom for trying to take a pee and you're worried that I'm going to turn out to be John Freaking Dillinger on the lam in drag? Get a life.* I say nothing, of course, just look at him respectfully and bat my eyelashes until he thinks I'm probably making a pass at him, or the estrogen has fried my brain. He finally signs the papers, looking up at me as if he's discovered something in the back of the fridge from last year's hunting trip.

But I'm not done. I ask him about changing my Ohio birth certificate, which still lists me as male. He loftily informs me that the State of Ohio doesn't do that sort of thing. It turns out they want a record, "contemporaneous with my birth." He intones contemporaneous solemnly, all 120 pounds of him. I'd like to contemporaneous his geeky twit head, but right now he's my knight in shining armor because I have my name-change papers tucked under my arm. So, batting my lashes one last time, this time just to cheese him off, I exit stage left. Anyway, it's September, and if I don't get to school in time for registration, all my preferred courses will be closed out.

A guy holds the door for me at the elevator. As he gets in behind me, he casually asks, "So, how tall are you anyway, Miss?" Then he looks again, a lot closer. Clearly confused now, he's not sure if he has just been polite or if he's just made an ass of himself by holding the door and flirting with a guy in drag.

When I arrive at Cleveland State, I have to fill out the admission forms, including indicating my sex. Well, I guess I can start checking the *F* box. The student behind the counter is trying to be friendly. I've stopped by home to change into a pair of jeans and he doesn't look real close, thinks he's talking to the average guy, and asks, "You play any hoops?" As I consider the answer, he eyes my Admin Form, spots *Sex: F*, and looks up quickly. But by then, he's mine.

148

"Oh yeah. Love to. In the men's league last year, they considered me just a small forward. But in the Women's League this year, I got to play a Patrick Ewing sort of power center."

"Great," he replies without an ounce of enthusiasm. I want to ask him if we can go out and shoot baskets sometime, but he's already turning an interesting shade of green, so I leave for the registration lines. On the way I stop to sign up for student insurance, which they offer at a really good discount. Again, I have to declare and sign my sex. Only this time, I have to answer a whole barrage of questions: Have I ever been pregnant? Hmmm... Let me think. Have I ever had an abortion? Not knowingly. Do I need information on birth control pills? Not unless my surgeon is a lot better than I think he is. But who knows? A good girl scout is always prepared, so I check that one *Yes*. Maybe now I'll find out where you insert those little pink pills.

It's on the way to the Financial Aid Office that I become aware I have to pee. This is always the most complex part of the day. Getting a sex-change is easier than negotiating the public toilet system. Which is worse—a woman in the men's room in heels using the urinal, or a man in the women's room using a stall? It's a toss-up. I make a beeline for the Women's Room.

Naturally, there's a line. I have to stand there, pretending ignorance of all the stares. Although half the women in line are more butch and gender-variant than I am, I'm half a head taller than anyone else. What can I say—a swan among the platypuses draws attention.

Someone asks me the time, which is usually a voice check. I see that she is wearing a watch herself, and she's closely examining my face, along with three of her friends. The rest of the line is casually watching while trying to look like they're not watching. I'm tempted to shift into low gear here and use my truckdrivin' growl, but I need a stall, not a scene. I answer in my highest and most petite voice. They ain't convinced, but at least they conclude I'm not the Mad Cleveland Bathroom Rapist stalking their restroom.

Once in the cubicle, I sit. But then, I notice I'm making more noise than anyone else. They're all swooshing and I'm splashing like a fire hose against a kettle drum at close range. When I'm done, I pass on fluffing before the mirror and beat a hasty retreat. Discretion is the better part of gender valor. On my way out, a dyke smiles indulgently. Mon amie!

At the student aid office, still more forms for loans, for the minimum-wage on-campus job they're throwing in to sweeten the package, and for more insurance in case I croak in school so the loan is retired. Each time I have to record and declare my sex. Why do they need my sex on a loan? Do penises pay differently? Am I going to sit on the money or something so that what's between my legs makes a difference? When I have a vagina, will they raise my interest rate?

The registration lines still reach halfway across the gym. But in short order, I'm done. It's almost 5:00 and time to go. I stop off at the library for some books I'll need for the first day of classes. Too much Coke while waiting in lines and again I need a bathroom.

Uh-oh. This time there are two CSU campus cops in their brown uniforms right outside the door. This is a city campus, and they're fully armed these days. The whole thing flashes in my mind like an old George Raft movie:

Cop 1: "All right, Miss, step away from that door!"

Cop 2: "Look out, Charlie! She's got a dick!"

Cop 1: "Don't move, Miss! Okay, put both balls on top of your head. Now lay your dick on the floor, and kick it over here... slowly!"

I can't handle another situation right now. I need to get busted for Public Impersonating like I need a hemorrhoid. I'll bear the pain until I get home. A young kid on the subway, noticing I'm carrying a load of books, offers me his seat. Chivalry isn't dead. Then his friend elbows him and whispers and they both look at me again and start to crack up. Chivalry hits the floor, colder'n a mackerel.

That's the easy part. The hard way is getting past the guys hanging around the corner near my house. It's usually not too bad, only they don't seem to know my name. One of them thinks I'm someone called Mary Cohen. No, wait, it's *maricon*. Another calls me *putah*. They do this every time I walk by. So far nothing physical has come of it, but I'm waiting and I'm also well prepared. I'm well prepared to hysterically cry my head off the first time one of them so much as touches me; then I'll hit them with a full load of Jewish guilt. After that they won't want to live.

I have a date tonight with Kris, my sweetheart. Contemplating this makes the day behind much more bearable. She comes by at eight, and we go to our favorite gay bar. The music is awesome. While I go to snag some brewskies, another woman comes up to her and says, "You know, that's really a guy you're with."

Kris just smiles sweetly. As if mulling over this new information, she begins thoughtfully scratching her chin with her middle finger. Later that night she muses aloud if my surgery will, "finally make an honest lesbian of me." Who knows? What are labels, anyway? Nothing but whole-body condoms to protect us from making intimate contact with each other.

What If They Gave a Sex, and Nobody Came?

Sex! It's a cultural command that all bodies understand and they recognize themselves in a specific way. It's an identification of our bodies that we are forced to carry around and produce on demand. To participate in society, we must be sexed.

We see this with perfect clarity in the case of the intersexed, the original lost brigade in any discussion of binary sex. Intersexuals are not permitted to live without a sex. Even if they resist, society inevitably forces one on them. The machinery of sex gets very upset when you try to live outside of it.

I have a friend who is raising his first child. He is determined to raise it without a sex until it is old enough to select its own. In the meantime, he tells me he cannot believe the incredible intensity of the daily cultural pressure he gets to sex his child. From the person at the checkout stand who asks, "Is that a boy or a girl?" to the insistent hospital records office which absolutely requires a sex, to salespeople in the kiddy clothing stores, to the forthcoming battles with nursery school officials.

There is an entire social apparatus whose sole purpose is to determine, track and maintain my sex.

Perhaps sex is not a noun at all. Perhaps it is really a verb, a cultural imperative—as in, "Sex yourself!"—in the face of which, none of us has a choice.

The Menace in Michigyn
(First appeared in the August, 1994 issue of the Village Voice)

Last night's rain is gone, and the afternoon sun is burning off the haze. We cross a red clay county road separating our tents from the wood posts, wire fences, and candy-colored tents of the Michigan Womyn's Music Festival. There are six of us, gender outlaws all, queued up like so many tenpins before the smiling woman in the ticket booth. The Michigan Womyn's Music Festival is about to meet the Transexual Menace.

This rather outlandish moment had its genesis in the summer of 1991. A transwoman, Nancy Jean Burkholder, was accosted by security guards near this very gate. The producers—Barbara ("Boo") Price and Lisa Vogel—stated a policy of "womyn-born womyn only." They interpreted this to exclude transwomen, and had Nancy evicted.

It's unlikely the participants in that anonymous late-night drama anticipated the chain reaction it would ignite. Within days, women across the country were talking about the eviction. In "Of Catamites and Kings," theorist and activist Gayle Rubin called it "the cause célèbre" of the '91 Festival. As Rubin writes, "After decades of feminist insistence that women are 'made, not born', after fighting to establish that 'anatomy is not destiny,' it is astounding that ostensibly progressive events can get away with discriminatory policies based so blatantly on recycled biological determinism."

In fact, the complexities of lesbian politics have always made the Borgias look like Ozzie and Harriet. And lesbian transphobia was hardly unique to Michigan. As early as 1972, a transwoman was forced out of the prototype lesbian organization, Daughters of Bilitis, and as recently as 1991 the National Lesbian Conference banned "nongenetic women." But the festival is one of the country's oldest and most visible gatherings of lesbians, with seven to 8,000 attendees each year. For many transsexuals, as well as the larger world, it is a unique symbol of lesbian culture. More importantly, the festival is closely identified with radical lesbian separatists, feminists who embrace Mary Daly's and Janice Raymond's theory that transsexual women are merely (I am not making this up) *surgically-altered men created by patriarchal surgeons to co-opt women's bodies and invade women's space*. For these reasons, the decision to admit "womyn-born womyn only" carried a special sting.

There have always been lesbians opposed to women appointing themselves "gender police," judging who can call themselves female and deciding which queer identities are deemed acceptable. "Despite theoretically embracing diversity," notes Gayle Rubin in *Deviations: A Gayle Rubin Reader*, "contemporary lesbian culture has a deep streak of xenophobia [responding with] hysteria, bigotry, and a desire to stamp out the offending messy realities. A 'country club syndrome' sometimes prevails in which the lesbian community is treated as an exclusive enclave from which the riff-raff must be systematically expunged."

Lesbians in early feminist consciousness-raising groups were told they weren't "real women." Butch-femme and S/M lesbians have been attacked for invading women's space with oppressive, patriarchal influence. The result has been an ongoing struggle within the lesbian-feminist world against the politics of exclusion. In this spirit, the posse accompanying six gender queers into this festival's bucolic vortex in 1994 included '60s stone butch Leslie Feinberg, '70s feminist Minnie Bruce Pratt, S/M sex outlaws from the '80s, the '90s answer to Queer Nation, and the Lesbian Avengers. What earthly power could stand against such a formidable and unholy alliance?

I could trace my own presence in Michigan back to 1978, when I began divesting the male trappings forced on me from birth, transitioning into someone cisgenders could recognize as female. In the process, my female lover and I metamorphosed from another nice, straight couple to a couple of militant *ho-mo-seck-choo-alls* walking arm-in-arm in broad daylight down the main streets of Cleveland Heights, Ohio.

How is a transwoman a lesbian? I can no more explain it than breathing, no more describe it than a smell. How is anyone a lesbian, except that she identifies as a woman and is attracted to women? Even before surgery made such things possible, desire had long since etched my dreams with soft butches and strong arms, their weight on my back and their insistent, taxing presence inside me. In all this I was not alone, for of 13 transgender women in Camp Trans, 11 were lesbian-identified.

So I knew the name for what I was, and I knew I belonged with other lesbians. But the women's community greeted us less like prodigal sisters returned to the fold than like the unchanged kitty litter. Following a decade of fruitless efforts to claim my place in the lesbian movement, and sick of being harassed at parties, in bars, and groups, I left for good. What was the point of tossing back brewskies with my oppressors, or fighting for a liberation which excluded the likes of me?

During the years of my premature retirement, transwomen (and men) began finding their own voices. Along with this newfound pride came outrage at our relentless oppression. Activist organizations with names like Transgender Nation and The Transexual Menace have sprung up across the country. We've zapped the Gay Games, Stonewall 25, various startled city councils, and the *Village Voice*.

So news of Nancy's expulsion from Michigan reached my ears like a gunshot across the water. I looked at the last 16 years of my life and considered my interminable struggles on the fringe of the lesbian community. Then I put on sensible shoes and headed toward the sounds of battle.

I joined them in 1993, after Nancy and three trans friends had again attempted to attend the festival. And security again had asked them to leave, maintaining that radical separatists were threatening violence, and that their safety on the land could not be guaranteed. When S/M women (many of whom were demonstrably more genderqueer than we were) stepped forward to insure their safety, security asserted the producer's "womyn-born womyn only" policy and insisted the transsexual women leave. The four women did, but we refused to pack up and go home. Instead, we set up camp directly across from the main gate and lobbied our case with anyone who would listen. Camp Trans was born, and in four days over 200 festival goers stopped by to offer support, food, water—and attend two impromptu workshops.

Camp Trans was about to become a staple of the Michigan festival, with or without official sanction.

In June of 1994, a fund-raiser was held in New York. For the first time, a transsexual event drew mainstream gay organizations, from the Lesbian Avengers to the Gay and Lesbian Alliance Against Defamation, along with mainstream queer activists like Ann Northrop, Minnie Bruce Pratt, and Amber Hollibaugh. If there is such a thing as a queer *Weltanschauung*, it was definitely moving in our direction.

Over $5,000 was pledged to send a bunch of gendertrash rejects to the Michigan woods. Plans were laid to fly nationally recognized queer activists from around the country for 25 workshops between August 10th and 14th, when attendance at the festival would peak. Two thousand schedules were printed and distributed as part of our plan to draw as many women as possible to Camp Trans ("for humyn-born humyns").

So now it is Saturday afternoon and our workshops—including the first annual "Mary Daly Memorial Volleyball Game: Surgically-Altered She-Male Scum vs. the World"—have drawn over 400 festigoers. One is Hillary Smith, a Lesbian Avenger from Portland, Oregon, and she, bless her subversive little heart, has recognized my Transexual Menace T-shirt. "Didn't I see you at an Avengers' meeting in Manhattan? Why don't you come to the national meeting inside?"

"Sure," I snap back, "why don't you just send me some escorts?"

"How many?", she replies, not missing a beat.

We have checked with Festival Security about this, and been told that Boo and Lisa's "womyn-born womyn only" policy stands. Unlike past years, however, each of us must interpret it for ourselves. And that is how the six of us—three transwomen and one intersex individual, Cody—happen to be here. I suspect our lives and identities are far more complex than any policy could possibly anticipate. I also suspect our grinning, excited escorts are enjoying this more than ducks in a rainstorm.

I love these strong women, but suddenly the idea that we need protection feels surreal and sad. There are sounds of nervous laughter, bad jokes, and a lot of affection going down the 40-person chain. I am wide-eyed; I have wanted to go to Michigan since 1978, and I am seeing it for the first time. Mostly, it's just acres and acres of forest, tents, campsites, and women looking up with reactions as varied as they are: astonishment, confusion, laughter, applause, raised fists, smiles, angry glares, indifference.

After what seems like forever, we head up a short rise to the Avengers' meeting area. This is the first time a mainstream, national lesbian group has supported transsexual women, and the scattered applause, growing to a real ovation as we come into full view, is an incredible rush. I have never seen so many young, hip dykes with good hair and straight teeth in one place and they are all, for gosh sakes, clapping for *us*.

Afterwards, fearing an angry confrontation for

which we will undoubtedly be blamed, there is general consensus that, having done what we came for, we ought to just declare victory and get the hell out of Dodge. I prefer Hillary's suggestion: go to the kitchen area and sit down and eat, just like we're normal people and belong there, which, damn it, we do. We compromise: march back out, crossing the packed kitchen area at dinnertime.

Coming around a bend, I see an opening about the size of a football field with, I don't know, 800, a thousand, who knows how many women in it. For a moment, it looks like the entire lesbian nation is spread out, eating, carrying food, leading children, or serving dinner. One woman, dressed entirely in studded chains and leather and sporting an enormous black strap-on, is cavorting along our path. She is going wild as we approach, and I stride up, grasping her dildo firmly and ask "Excuse me, can we talk?" I see women all over turning now to stare at us, and, my palms suddenly moist, I breathe, "We are going to fucking die."

You think people's mouths only drop open in cartoons or sitcoms, but I assure you their jaws actually do go slack in real life. As we're walking, festigoers see us, momentarily freeze, then just as abruptly spring back to life, trying to grok who and what we are. Applause breaks out, the odd raised fist, a few waves, and finally lots and lot of smiles. Almost without exception, these women support our cause. By now we are all beaming as well; I am grinning like an idiot at anyone within range. I am suddenly aware, clearly and precisely, that lesbian politics is changing—fundamentally, irrevocably, right before my eyes.

How do I feel? Being transsexual is like a tax: you pay it to get a job, rent an apartment, find a lover, just exist. Phrases like *women-born women only, biological women only, genetic women only*, or whatever exclusionary formula is in vogue, cut deeply. With each hurt I hear anew Alice Walker's admonition never to be the only one in the room, and recall that as a transwoman, I am usually the only one in the room.

But not today. Today I have sisters: protecting me, standing beside me, honoring my presence. Mostly being here feels just like coming home.

Our Cunts Are *NOT* the Same

From time to time I do a workshop I first performed at Camp Trans, "Our Cunts Are Not the Same: Transsexual Sexuality and Sex-Change Surgery." I gratefully credit the idea to Annie Sprinkle, from whom I unblushingly stole it. Annie does a hands-on fist-fucking segment, as well an "examine my cervix" portion, in her performance art. She was kind enough to share some of her tips with me on how to carry such a thing off.

The first half is comfortingly didactic. I discuss the various techniques and technologies of surgery. I describe what it feels like. I use lots of medical terms. Everyone seems at ease. They ask intelligent, sensitive questions. I try to give intelligent, sensitive answers.

Then I tell them we are moving from the theoretical to the experiential. This portion I lovingly refer to as the Show'n'Tell, Touch'n'Feel, or sometimes, Scratch'n'Sniff.

Drop Your Drawers: It's Going to Be a Bumpy Ride

I drop my drawers. Since, unlike Annie, I am not an artiste and I don't get paid for this, everyone who wants to stay drops their drawers, as well. At Camp

Trans, we had about two dozen people. We thought maybe three or four might stick around. Since it was my first time, that was fine with me. It was all I felt I could handle.

We were wrong. You could have gone deaf from the sound of jeans hitting the deck. To my horror, even single one of them stayed, and all were looking expectantly, trustingly at me.

At the National Women's Music Festival, held annually in Bloomington, Indiana, we had the opposite reaction. Several people were trampled in the rush for the door. Luckily, I got to administer mouth-to-mouth. No matter. Again, about two dozen intrepid souls were left when the dust cleared and Science continued its relentless march onward. Neither snow, nor rain, nor dark of night can stop me from getting felt up by 20 women.

For the Scratch'n' Sniff, everyone pulls on latex gloves (safe sex only) and gets to feel a real live transgender vah-jay-jay. It's no big deal for me; I do it all the time. But for them it's a different matter.

Several interesting things occur, the least of which is that people fall apart. For many women, this is a gut-wrenching experience. It's one thing to talk about sex-change surgery, argue about whether I'm a "real woman," and all that jazz. It's another entirely to find your hand buried to the knuckles inside the warm, breathing body of another person—to feel the heat, the skin of a vagina, watching hips move if you hit the right place.

This matter with hips has occasionally gotten, so-to-speak, out of hand. I sometimes forget I am among lesbians. It usually begins as an experiment. One woman hits that certain spot, my hips turn, and before you can say, "read my lips," all of them are trying it. Pretty soon, I feel more like the losing end of lesbian target practice than a show'n'tell exhibit. Then some girl gets the smart idea of seeing if she can make me moan a little. Then someone tries to make me moan a lot. I have to call a halt to the proceedings here; after all, we're scientists, not sluts.

At Bloomington, the lover of one participant accused her partner of infidelity because she had fucked me. Explanations that this was Science, that it was nonsexual, even that I wasn't really another female, were to no avail.

Another participant discovered her friends from home were so grossed out that she had touched a transgender cunt, "a man's cunt!" (I don't make'em up, folks, I just report 'em), that they stopped speaking to her. She related all this to me through tears, because these were people she had come to the Festival with and had known since childhood. She was astonished to discover how transphobic they were towards me, and correspondingly quick to turn on her, as if I were contagious. What was even stranger was that her outraged friends were so deliciously and completely butch, they made me feel like I was an extra Southern Belle in lace and petticoats straight from *Gone with the Wind*.

A non-participant, who had read of the workshop in the festival's schedule of events, was so offended by the idea that she wrote a scathing letter to the board. It was caustic and rich in feminist invective. And it probably would have been effective, too, except that the board member to whom it was addressed had not only had her own hand in me up to the wrist (ouch!), but had also taken it upon herself to assay an unscheduled excursion up my asshole as well, something I was quickly and loudly constrained to point out was not on our afternoon's trip-tik adventure.

But What a DEEP Penis You Have, Grandma!

Another interesting thing happens when I challenge all participants, in the strongest terms possible, to refer to the area in question as a penis and not a vah-jay-jay. I remind them that many transgender vaginas are actually constructed by inverting the penis, so I say that I would prefer that they refer to mine by its original name.

It's not important that that is not the particular surgery I had. The point is that if so many cisgender lesbian feminists still consider us men, and deny that our bodies are "women's bodies," then let them call it a penis. Fair enough, if you have those beliefs, let's take them to their logical conclusion. And not theoretically or politically, that's too cheap, but right here, right now—flesh-on-flesh.

No surprise, no one is able to do it. Nearly all the participants do three things: first, they exclaim about the wonders of modern surgery; second, they invariably refer to it as a "cunt" or "vagina;" and, third, they declaim about how it's "just like" theirs.

I have come to understand that some very active visual and semiotic construction is going on. It's simply impossible, it seems, for festival participants to relate to my genitals as other than a vagina.

It is true that we tend to organize our visual field into familiar signs, especially something as fundamental and visceral as genitals. What would someone say to understand and eroticize my crotch: "Oh, I just love this penis, and I'd love to stick my tongue deep down inside it?" This is just not an erotically (or semiotically) intelligible statement. The only way to understand my genitals is through reinscribing them as a cunt. (Of course, since this is exactly what many transwomen want. I have no moral or religious objections to it either.)

Frankly My Dear, I Don't Give a Damn

But what of Holly Boswell? Holly is a delicate Southern belle of long acquaintance. I may occasionally feel like an extra from *Gone With the Wind*, but Holly actually is one. S/he has tender features—long, wavy blond hair, a soft Carolina accent, a delicate feminine bosom—and no interest in surgery.

Holly lives as an openly transgendered mother of two in Asheville, North Carolina. Her comforting advice to confused citizens struggling with whether to use *Sir* or *Madam* is, "Don't give it a second thought. You don't have a pronoun yet for me." This goes over famously with the gentle folk of the Deep South.

Now, just between you and me, I confess that, for some time now, I have had this killer crush on Holly's tender flesh. We've chatted about this together, engaging in a lot of half-hearted flirting and affectionate banter when our paths have crossed at various gender conventions. What we have also discussed, and what is even more interesting for me, is the question Holly's body poses. If she ever took my banter seriously and we became involved, what would I do with her body?

Just Hand Me That Collar on the Nightstand, Will You?

It is not at all clear what Holly's body means to me. For starters, how would I eroticize her penis? Would I treat it as a big clit? Or as a penis? Or would I have to find some completely new meaning? In fact, I'm unclear how Holly herself conceives of or would prefer her genitals to be eroticized.

I don't suppose I should really need to have any particular meaning for her body at all, except that for most of us, eroticism is connected in some fundamental way to very gendered qualities with which we imbue bodies : virility, softness, hairiness, strength, vulnerability, and so on. This tells me that gender, that notorious difference engine, is hard at work here, defining and delimiting what things count as erotic.

For me to eroticize Holly, particularly her genitals, requires that I do some quick, intense reinscribing. It is obvious to me that her inscription of what her penis means does not match my own idea of what penises mean. To negotiate sex between us would therefore mean negotiating new meanings. In fact, I'm not sure she self-identifies as such, but she is not only trans and genderqueer, but what is increasingly known as "nonbinary," and that tends to scramble most of what we think about male-female bodies because it is, well, not binary.

The idea of negotiating erotic meanings can lead to interesting situations. For example, how do we eroticize those always-absent bodies: intersex bodies, whose genital formations may be quite different from, or contain mixed features of, what we normally conceive of as genitals? What does a "large clit" or a "small penis," either one combined with a vaginal opening, mean? How do they challenge and subvert our understanding of eroticism?

And please do not refer me to arguments of "pathology" or "sexual function." It is manifestly the case that most some intersex bodies function perfect well sexually, and sometimes perhaps even better than ours or simply in ways we don't expect.

Transbodies and transgenitals create uncertainty and anxiety among many people. Straight men are afraid that by fucking transwomen they become gay. Straight women are confused about what to do with non-operative male transsexuals in bed. Married women are unsure of what to do with their husbands' penises under lace panties beneath silk dressing gowns. Gay men are confused by the appearance of "transfags"—transmen who are gay . Lesbians are conflicted about what it means to sleep with transwomen who still have penises or who may still have somewhat masculine characteristics. On the other hand, many lesbians are genuinely confused with their butch lovers who decide they're really transsexual men, start taking testosterone, growing beards, and "packing."

Activist (and, if personal experience is any guide, world-class sex pervert) Nancy Nangeroni has observed that all this confusion means many transpeople will spend most of their romantic lives alone. By crossing the lines of gender, you cross the lines of eroticism. You also cross the lines of aesthetics. Bodies which combine differently gendered parts, and displays often appear disconcerting, disturbing, ridiculous, or simply enigmatic to others. Finding a partner under these circumstances becomes much, much harder.

Loneliness, and the inability to find partners, is one of the best-kept secrets in the transcommunity. It's something many of us carry around like a private shame, a secret wound we hide from view. This is because we are convinced this isolation only confirms our deepest fears—that we are somehow deficient. Instead, it should remind us that, once again, the personal is political.

The gender system, which marks many kinds of bodies as either non-erotic or erotically problematic, is at work even in the most intimate spaces of our lives. We fall off the grid of erotic intelligibility which sections the body into known, recognizable parts. Transbodies are the cracks in the gender sidewalk. When we find partners, they must be willing to negotiate the ambiguity of the terrain.

One Imported Water and Two Designer Genitals To Go, Please

For years, I really hated this little spot on my body. I shared my concern in support groups and recovery meetings, sobbing and unable to hide my shame. It was a small portion of my penis. To create my clitoris, the doctor had transplanted the head of my penis between my newly formed lips, waited a few months, and then carved it down to look like a "real clitoris."

This fact that my glans had actually lived between my labia for nearly three months, humiliated me. I overate because of it. I tried to ignore my body when I self-recreated in the privacy of my own bedroom. Of course, it's much harder to masturbate, not to mention come, when you're tryin hard to ignore your body. But in my mind's eye, I could still see that glans, implanted like some rabid creature from *Alien,* about to burst out of my body to attack Sigourney Weaver.

Current practice in sex-change surgery assumes, even requires, "real-looking" genitals. Otherwise, what's the point? It also assumes, and even requires, that transpeople desire "real-looking" genitals. This is why so many doctors, while proudly showing off how "their vagina" can even fool Ob/gyns, are reduced to muttering darkly about "no guarantees" and "we can't be certain" when asked about the pleasure potential of their work. It's also part of why so many transwomen don't have a lot of erotic sensation after surgery. We don't ask too closely about how it feels so much as we ask how it will look.

This same medical obsession with looks is why so many intersex infants survive their non-consensual sex-change type surgeries with so little erotic sensation later in life. What are genitals, if they are not penises or cunts? We all want our groins to look just like real men's and women's, don't we, even if we must carve infants' flesh to achieve that all-important illusion?

And, of course, the only surgery most doctors will perform is one from column *A* or one from column *B*: there is no intermediate ground. But as transactivist Dana Priesing notes, if Nature naturally makes intersex people, then what could possibly be wrong with wanting to become intersex? In fact, why not bite the bullet and admit that intersex genitals, instead of being defective

169

versions of "the real thing," are often different, most interesting, or simply... better?

Logically, since surgery doesn't make one anything, nor does having a penis prevent one from being anything else, why can we not have "designer genitals?" I reasoned this before I'd heard of it in reality. I always knew transmen who undertook surgery attempted various kinds of penises, but various kinds of vaginas?

Then my friend Hannah approached me about having surgery. She was interviewing surgeons, and wondered how my surgery had been done. When we finished talking, she said she wanted to keep her entire glans and as much sensitivity as possible. She later polled her lesbian friends on how they would cope sexually with her new groin. True to form, they reconstructed the available erotic categories right onto her body without a blink, quickly declaring that it would be just a nice, big clit.

Interestingly, the well-known surgeon who performed the surgery, was willing to do so only under protest. He informed her it was mutilation (!?) and perversion. I am fairly confident he meant "perversion" here as a bad thing. Anyway, I suppose his idea was that wanting your penis sewn into a real looking vagina was "normal," but getting creative and inserting your own aesthetics into the process was not.

My Hannah stuck with it, staring back at him calmly and declaring that it was her body, her money, and this was what she wanted. Perversion or no, it was what she was going to get. He relented.

Who knows how the frontiers can be explored as we move forward? Suppose the market grows and the big design houses get directly involved. They already gladly put their logos on everything from pillowcases to cars, why not genitals? Maybe someday you'll be able to order a Gucci (continental, comes with matching shoes and handbag), a Bill Blass (very corporate "power" genitals), a Shelby-Cobra (high-torque penis with overhead cam, kick start, and 400 horsepower) or, for truly safe sex, a Volvo (roll it over and walk away without a scratch).

A Fascism of Meaning

Fluid Meanings

I am sitting through that obligatory, apparently interminable nightmare of the high school curriculum: the health and sciences class. But today, I will at last learn the secrets of those little delicate blue-lined drawings I found in my sister's dresser drawer, showing young women happily inserting various kinds of cardboard tubes into obscure orifices.

Yes, today we are to learn the mysteries of menstruating (*not* Menace-trating, which involves T-shirts and picketing and is a different thing altogether).

But wait, there's more! Yes, today we have the health and science double-feature. We're going to cover ejaculation. Now, ejaculation has been a real problem of mine for some time, because I seem to be doing a great deal of it lately. I have a book, *Sex for Teenagers: Frank Talk for Honest Questions*. It has this happy teen hetero couple on the cover, holding hands, looking brightly into each other's eyes and somehow managing to look both uncertain and frisky at once. And yes, it covers masturbation.

It says, "Most normal teenagers find it necessary to masturbate to completion from time to time." I've

172

read that part over about 20 times now, consulting it as if it were the Delphic Oracle. But what do they mean by *completion*? I mean, is that ejaculation, or does it mean merely stopping when you feel kind of finished? Maybe most normal teens feel completion right before the final act. Maybe, for them, just a few, good strokes in the shower is enough, and they feel completion, and, unlike certifiable perverts like me, they don't find it necessary to jerk off until they actually (yuck!) ejaculate.

On the now-critical subject of masturbation, it doesn't say a word about coming home from school, scrambling down into the basement and across the laundry room to lock yourself in the most distant bathroom in the house so you can add yet another handkerchief, wadded together like a cement sculpture, to the growing collection in the laundry hamper which by now surely your mother, the cleaning lady, or both must have noticed. In fact, I am convinced the only reason they haven't denounced me to the Sex Police and had me carted away is that, having graciously turned down all increases in my allowance, I'm very cheap to keep around. Moreover, because they—like most normal teens of their day—probably found it necessary to masturbate to completion from time to time, they're cutting me some slack.

But I don't know for sure, and there's no adult at hand I can readily ask. I mean, some evening over dinner, I can't chime in with, "Pass the carrots, would you Sis? Hey Dad, I was just wondering, did you or Mom ever masturbate *to completion* when you were kids?"

173

I'll Show You My Fluids If You Show Me Yours

So I am ready, even desperate, to learn today. And luckily for me, as Emily Martin notes in, *The Woman in the Body: A Cultural Analysis of Reproduction* (Boston: Beacon Press, 1992) Science seems to have pinned all this down pretty well.

It seems that menstruation entails the discharge from the body of a couple of teaspoons of lukewarm fluid. This discharge occurs about once a month for a number of years, and women's bodies lose perhaps 500 gametes slowly over about 40 years. This process is unfailingly described by both the scientific literature and the teacher in the most unambiguous terms of bodily waste, loss, weakness, and general femininity. Inevitably stressed is the loss of the cell, which, if it were only properly deployed, could have led to a live human being. The boys look over at the girls who are uniformly staring at the floor, aghast and ashamed at all the potential little human beings leaking out of their bodies, perhaps even at that moment.

We move on to ejaculation. This part is much better. It seems ejaculation entails the discharge from the body of a couple of teaspoons of lukewarm fluid. This discharge occurs—- oh, up to five times a day—- for a number of years, and men's bodies lose perhaps two gazillion (the number is imprecise here) gametes each time: little potential human beings sprayed into the carpet, handkerchiefs, rolled pieces of liver, hollowed-out pumpkins, almost anything you can name. No matter, I am gratified to note that this process is unfailingly described by both the scientific literature and the teacher in the most unambiguous

174

terms of virility, dominance, strength, potency, and general masculinity. The girls now stare over at the boys with open envy, while the boys themselves are lost in rapt contemplation of their own pubescent, potent crotches.

The teenage years that follow are both hard to remember and difficult to forget. They are filled with things I do not want to recall. All the boys trying on the cocksure walk of manhood: the knowing laugh, the rude gesture, the practiced invective; struggling to out-butch each other in the now-serious struggles for dominance, interspersed with occasional quick and violent fistfights; the running, seemingly endless commentary on intercourse in which the girl is inevitably "stacked."

The girls, for their part, do not resist this appropriation of their bodies, but instead accept it as natural. They become increasingly self-conscious of their own breasts and hips which have become a portal of vulnerability. A mere pointed gaze at these from any of us is enough to cause a tightened jaw, a quickened stride, or sometimes a flirtatious smirk. They begin to form their own complementary pecking order based largely on boy-popularity, breast size, good looks, and, of course, that indispensable quality—thinness.

All in all, everyone learns what their bodies are supposed to mean, how they are to act as they become the totally predictable people fate has in store.

For me, this meant becoming all boy, all of the time. It was a time of profound loss of self because there appeared to be no alternative, so that the whole thing seemed not so much something that was being done to me as the inevitable consequence of what I actually was. My body, which had been simply my body, became a place imbued with a confusing welter of meanings I was required to gain command of and navigate, in order to survive: all of them natural, and thus inescapable.

A Special Appropriation

Puberty is often described as a time when adolescents experience great anxiety, mood swings, and confusion due to hormonal and bodily changes. I propose a more pedestrian source for such behaviors: once society begins to "see" our pubescent bodies as potential surfaces for eroticism and procreation, their views descend upon us with all the subtlety of an iron fist.

Girls growing breasts, boys growing pubic hair and deeper voices, suddenly find they have to memorize and master an entire set of adult meanings. It is not just that things as static signs, like bodies, must mean certain things, but also that we must maintain a consonance between those meanings and our entire expressive language of possible clothing, gesture, and stance. This dressage of gender becomes a daily ritual and begins to dictate our lives and our interrelationships. Girls are brought down from the trees, boys from playing with the girls.

Adults begin to observe us—no longer to keep us from the dangers of crossing the street, but from the dangers of crossing gender rules. We, in turn, learn to observe ourselves and to police each other. Anyone who has been the subject of, or witness to, the taunting, ostracism, and intimidation visited by teens upon a genderqueer—the special venom and unique savagery—must wonder where they learned it. No wonder is necessary: we taught ourselves.

I remember seeing Diane Stein sunbathing in a two-piece swimsuit as I shot baskets in her backyard, and the sudden shaft of pain, of realization, that the lovely body she exposed to the sun was now as distant, as unobtainable for me as the planet Mars, and that a part of me was irrevocably lost. I don't know how many hours I've invested in the years since, trying to get back to whoever I was before that afternoon.

For the first time I learned shame: not shame for what I had or hadn't done, but shame for what I *was*. And for what I *knew*. The knowledge broke upon me anew each day in school. In order to survive, I was going to have to lie a great deal—to my parents, my teachers and my friends, and not just with my words, but with my body and my actions.

It was not just the back of my father's hand that I feared, or the beatings after school, or even the general ostracism, although that would have been more than enough, but a strange feeling that something else lurked out there for genderqueers which was truly dangerous. Something waited for me that ate little queers raw, and at the time, I didn't know what it was. For years I chalked it up to paranoia until I began to come across the phenomenon of Psychiatric Abuse of Gender-Variant Children (PAGC). These were stories of teenagers put on locked wards, subjected to involuntary therapy, and treated to round-the-clock behavior modification for being only marginally more genderqueer in their actions than I was in my heart.

Children don't own their own bodies. While we do not physically violate them, certainly we as a culture appropriate and control their bodies in nearly every other way. The shape and expression of each child's gender and sexuality is constantly monitored, policed, regulated and punished by parents, religious institutions, schools, etc. As a society we are obsessed with the mythical "innocence of childhood," yet when it comes to children's gender and sexuality, it is hard to escape the conclusion that adolescence is when our culture eats its young.

And if this whole process falls more heavily on transgendered and "pre-homosexual" children, if—as I increasingly suspect—it is all too often accompanied not by a metaphoric incest or sexual violation, but by a real and physical one, then it is only because, within this baroque system, genderqueer kids present an ideal profile for sexual predators. We are often emotionally transparent, hungry for adult attention and approval, out of touch with our own bodies, socially isolated, lacking in any sense of boundaries, confused about what is "normal," and used to keeping secrets about our bodies. If there are sharks in the water, the social thrashing of genderqueer kids is bound to attract them. Such abuse appears not as an anomaly, but as a cultural norm: the means by which genderqueer kids are instructed in the limits and consequences of gender difference.

The Body as a Site of Constraint and Authorization

What has become apparent is that my physical person—its perceived properties, size, weight, curvature—has been pressed into service by society as a site of *constraint* and *authorization*. Constraint, because some meanings are disallowed me by my own flesh. Authorization, because having certain characteristics authorizes me—obliges me—to feel certain things, to have a particular sense of myself. I suspect that the issue is not so much freeing my "self" as uncovering the ways in which this particular self is a product of culture—again, an historical item, as much as the clothes I wear or the books I read. Just like them, it was created, distributed, and promoted in responses to highly specific, if diffuse, cultural needs.

I am reminded of a friend I spoke with whom I addressed as a woman. She'd been considering surgery between bouts of crossdressing and deep depression. She responded that she could not ever possibly be a woman, since she had a big belly, hairy arms, and a penis. I responded that that was exactly the kind of woman I liked. She broke down in tears.

If human beings were forced to march from one person to another, announcing things about themselves that made them feel dreadful, or made to carry signs inscribed with the painful words, we would instantly recognize this as a terrible assault. But what about a system that uses the body itself as a text to announce certain things? What about the large-breasted woman, for example, who feels that, whenever she enters a room, her body is forced to say, "I am sexually provocative and sensuous?" If you happen to wear a 44-D cup, you are going to have to constantly pull uphill against what your breasts are perceived to be saying to the world.

The use of bodies to constrain or authorize various meanings and feelings doesn't affect only transpeople. Why is it okay in this society to be "fat

179

and lazy," or "fat and jolly," but not "fat and sexy?" Why is it that fat people often have tremendous difficulty seeing themselves as sexy, or, if they do, are not allowed to display that meaning? If people perceive you as fat, try walking out the door in New York City in a low-cut blouse, short skirt, and high heels and see if you can make it to the subway without being humiliated.

In my case, I was constrained from feeling things about my body and obliged to feel others. I was denied access to the broad range of non-verbal language with which we express our sense of self: in posture, gesture, clothing, adornment, and inflection. This, in turn, helped constrain what I actually felt, for, as anyone knows, it is a difficult maneuver to feel something and simultaneously refrain from expressing it non-verbally. Visibility can be a trap.

To avoid displaying any of the "inappropriate" and prohibited signs about myself, I policed myself from feeling them, lest I give myself away with a gesture, a stance, or anything that would allow others to smell that *something* about me was not right, that would single me out and make me a target for social retribution. Most times I succeeded; sometimes, I failed. At certain junctures I didn't need to police myself; there didn't seem to be any choice. I acted masculine in some circumstances not because I was forced to, but because that seemed, in some inexpressible way, to be what I was, and, since there was pretty much universal agreement about it, acting otherwise was unthinkable.

In general, I got better and better at hiding my feelings deeper and farther away, until they were completely hidden, even from me. And a good bit of my life is now given over to a kind of introspective archaeology, where I try to unearth and piece together parts of myself lost to antiquity. Each discovery, like the surfacing of a hidden incident of childhood abuse or violation, brings with it fresh pain and fresh tears and still, even at my age, a surprisingly robust and irrational sense of fear.

A Fascism of Meaning

All of which is pretty ridiculous, since meanings do not cling to bodies like some kind of glutinous vapor or semiotic paste. On the contrary, every meaning attaching to our bodies was put there by someone, long ago. Every gendered scar on my psyche has distinctly cisgender fingerprints, and they show up with the lightest dusting and in the poorest light.

These are crimes, but they are small, silent, daily crimes, and the ensuing screams are swallowed in a vacuum. They are not crimes of passion, but crimes of meaning, the imposition of a kind of "fascism of meaning" which robs us of our bodies at an early age and bids us recognize ourselves, and be perpetually recognized, in very specific ways. In effect, we require dominance/power displays of our men, and submission/vulnerability displays of our women. And to speed them in fulfilling this universal cultural requirement, we construct male bodies as meaning dominance and power, and female bodies as meaning submission and vulnerability. It is as coercive and un-consenting as being named, and infinitely more indelible.

For some people, this pressure is like a vise, and it squeezes them until nothing is left. I have observed people who walk into trans-support groups, only to be left speechless, sitting through entire meetings in mute silence. And I am reminded of a close intersex friend, a particularly brilliant, charming, and resourceful person who, when I inquired after her obvious difficulty navigating even the most basic social situations, replied, "Well, you know, I lived the first 20 years of my life in a brown paper bag."

In the midst of this punishing system, I have also seen the most astonishing resilience and dignity on faces, a buoyancy and survivorship transcending circumstance. I suspect this is because at heart we, in all our messy complexity, are much more stubborn and rude and resourceful than the political system which seeks to invest us with shame.

The Search for Resonance

To navigate in a society of human beings, to *think oneself* at all, one must have a self: a specific organization of flesh, soul, and meaning, a mental sign which stands for "this person," having certain properties and characteristics.

In *The Straight Mind and Other Essays* (Boston: Beacon Press, 1992), theorist Monique Wittig observed that "...the first, the permanent, and the final social contract is language." Our bodies—as signs in that language—are the first and most permanent element of that linguistic contract, and in order to participate in the social space of language, we agree to be our "selves" as we are seen by others, that is, our particular physical selves—fat or thin, black or white, young or old. The most basic part of that linguistic contract to which our bodies are apprenticed is to be sexed, and being sexed in this context does not mean agreeing to mouth the words "I am female," to answer to the name, or to mark the box next to *Male* with an *X*. It means agreeing to feel and look and act your sex, to participate in society as a meaningful member within the matrix of expectations that go along with your sex.

If it is true that, at this point in human development, we must have a "self." Perhaps the single most profound and private thing we can create on our journey through this life is our sense of who and what we are. This is not a problem for most of us. We inherit meanings for ourselves which are more or less acceptable.

For others, the self which resonates within us is entirely at odds with what culture works to inscribe on our flesh. And this inaugurates a lifelong battle. To be so taxed with a cultural body whose meanings not only fail to resonate, but which actively militate against our deepest sense of what is meaningful, consequential, and true at every turn, to have this experience is to feel a unique kind of discomfort and pain. It affords little respite. For it is not just that it is there in the shower, in dating situations, before strangers on the street, when applying for a job, undressing, in the act of making love, and in the eyes of family and friends, but it is also in our heads, whenever we think about what constitutes "me."

When I refused to acquiesce, when I fought back, persisting in my insubordination, I was obliged to occupy that gender gulag, that spare, oblique wasteland known as *transgender*. And please don't tell me we're

183

going to resuscitate the term so that I can inhabit it with comfort and newfound pride. I am not interested in taking up residence in forced housing no matter how nicely it's dressed up for the occasion. I'm also not interested in the "freedom" to self-identify within a host of ready-made, off-the-rack social constructs.

Nor am I interested in those supposedly more sophisticated solutions seeking to locate my identity as falling somewhere along a marvelous "spectrum of gender," one inevitably anchored and dominated by identities which aren't my own. I have too often been obliged to speak my name in and through the political category of *transgender*, because, as I was told, people like me transgressed gender, when it is manifestly the case that it is gender which has transgressed all over me.

What I *am* interested in is access to distinctly different ways of organizing my self, which do not first require that I have such and such a kind of body or sexuality in order to be heard, which do not require of me that I have any specific identity at all in order to participate.

CLICK. Hello?

CLICK
   Hello?

   Yes. Hello, I'm a transsexual woman and I ...
   CLICK
   Hello? Hello?

   Yes. Hello, I'm interested in changing the sex on
my driver's ...
   CLICK
   Hello? Hello?

   Yes. Hi. I'm just your normal female woman and
I notice they've made a mistake on my driver's
license, ha-ha, and put me down, ha-ha, wait till you
get this, as a man. Can you tell me how I can get this
changed? What?.... I'll have to bring my birth
certificate down with my correct sex on it so you can
verify it? Okay.
   CLICK

   Hello? County Records Office? I'm a transsexual
and I ...
   CLICK

Hello? Hello?

Yes? County Records Office? I'm trying to get my driver's license corrected. You see, it lists me as a man and they told me to get it changed. I have to get a copy of my birth certificate and...
CLICK
Hello? Hello?

County Records? Yes. I'm just your average woman here in the county, and yesterday, just looking through some old papers, I noticed a couple of errors on my birth certificate and I was just kind of wondering, you know, woman-to-woman here, how I could get them corrected.... Uh huh... submit a doctor's statement contemporaneous with my birth from the attending physician or else a notarized statement from my current personal physician and a second notarized statement from a physician here in the county of origin? Thank you.
CLICK

Yes. Doctor's Office? I'd like to speak with ...
Please hold, Sir.
CLACK
...
...
...
CLICK

Hello, Doctor's Office? Yes I just called. Please don't put me on ...
Can you hold please, Sir?

CLACK

...

...

CLICK

Yes. I've been put on hold twice. Can I please talk to Dr. Sprocket?

I'm connecting you now, Sir.

Doctor Sprocket? This is Riki Wilchins. Right. I know you've only seen me a couple of times but now that I've started hormones and everything I'm having trouble finding work as a woman and I need to change

...

CLONCK

Hello? Hello?

Yes. Doctor? Yes, well, we were cut off. As I was saying, I'm trying to change my driver's license so I can get a job but they want my birth certificate and that's still male so I have to get that changed and to do that I'll need a statement from you that—no, I can't take time off from work to come in to see you.... Well, first, I can't because I have no job to take time from and second because I can't afford another $150 visit— no, I'm not trying to be difficult.... Yes, I know surgeons are very busy and they save lives and all but.... Look if you could please just see your way clear to...

CLICK

Hello? Hello? Doctor? Doctor Sprocket? Yes. I'm sorry I got angry, Doctor. Look, is there any way you could sign a statement that I'm female so I can get my paperwork done and get a job? ...I know you can't be certain yet, but how many men want to take estrogen and grow bosoms? ...Oh, really? I had no idea.... Yes, I know I still sleep with women and that's not very normal for a transsexual.... No, I haven't looked very feminine when I've come for my appointments.... Well, have you ever tried walking around the city in a push-up bra, pantyhose, 3-inch heels, and—Oh, really? I had no idea.... Well then you know what I—No, I wasn't aware you wear women's panties under your smock when you operate, but I can certainly sympathize with—What? You want me to see what? ...Who? ...Is there anyway we could avoid this.... Okay. Okay, yes. I'm sure you're looking out for my interests. Goodbye.

CLICK

Hello? Hello? Dr. Farvis? Dr. Francis Farvis? Yes. This is Riki Wilchins. Yes. That's right... from Dr. Sprocket. Yes, Thursday is fine... afternoon is fine. How much?... You said how much?? Is that absolutely necessary?.... Okay, okay. Yes, I want to get my paperwork done.... Yes, I'll be there at 4:00 p.m. sharp.... No, believe me, Doctor, it won't be any trouble getting off work.... No, I haven't been in therapy before.... Yes, I'll try to come properly dressed. Speaking of which, did you know that Dr. Sprocket—no, never mind, just thinking out loud.... Yes, I know thinking out loud could be a sign of— Well, of course I sound a little agitated and defensive, Doctor! Now let me ask you a question. Do you have any idea at all how frustrating it can be jumping

through all these humiliating hoops and having to beg random people for their help just so you can get a sex change operation and—Oh really? I had no idea. Yes... yes... okay, I'll see you Thursday. Goodbye, Doctor.
CLICK

Hello? City Courts. Yes. I'm a transsexual woman and I need to get my name changed and...
CLICK
Hello? Hello?

Lines in the Sand, Cries of Desire

We are the women who like to come, and come hard.
~ Amber Hollibaugh

In your face, Joan, in your face.

We spoke last week, just your average phone call. And then, as we're ringing off, you suggest I might want to write about the boundaries where my different selves meet: the complexity of this place, its borders and contours. Your suggestion leaves my face burning with shame and anger as if I had been struck. Who has ever wanted to hear such things? Where on earth can a lesbian, a pre-operative transsexual with a cock, a woman, a femme, an addict, an incest survivor, and a post-operative transsexual with a cunt intersect? Upon what map is it drawn?

I have spent my life exploring the geography of this place, mastering unfamiliar terrain and alien customs, wandering regions as fresh, as uncharted, as inexplicable to me as private visions. I have surveyed its pathways, as ignorant and blind as any first-time explorer, and finally discovered myself at day's end—lost, alone, bewildered, and afraid. With time, my tracks have intersected and converged, crisscrossed again and again, until at last they have woven their own pattern: my life

190

itself has become the place where these different selves meet, my skin the boundary that contains them, the women in my life the bordering states.

You say you want me to tell you about this place, its complexities and desires, its contours and terrain. It is 1:00 a.m.on Sunday morning, and at the moment I am more involved with the contours and terrain of the cock dangling about two inches before my face. I am 42, and I have been coming to this mostly straight, couples-only sex club in mid-Manhattan for almost a year now, working my way through acts successively more challenging and frightening for me, pushing back the boundaries of what I can do or imagine, practicing with newfound skill staying present and connected during sex, exorcising demons and ghosts by now so familiar I know their names and faces within an environment so anonymous I often don't know those of my partners. It is a place where straightforward sex is the commodity, physical beauty the currency, and lust the only coin. This is the ground I have chosen to confront my deep fear of butch or masculine sexuality, of possession and surrender, power and vulnerability, where I can finally recover the many, the myriad ways and fragments of my life lost to incest, transsexuality, shame and self-hate. I am trying to reclaim myself, and I want my body back.

I want my body back.

I want my clit, my scrotum, my vagina, my cock, my beard. My buttocks, my thighs, my bush, my asshole, my urethra, my semen. My lips, my tongue, my wetness, and my saliva. I want my breasts back, the ones I watched go through a second complete puberty at 29. I want my nipples back, with the scars just beneath my pink areolae where the implants went in, the left incision making the nipple over my heart mostly numb to touch or tongue. I want the scar on my throat, the one people notice and ask about my thyroid condition, the one opened to shave my Adam's apple down. And I want the scars you can't see, on the inside of my labia, the ones you get by doing the stitching from the inside, so they don't show. The ones which ache when I'm getting ill and itch strangely when I'm getting exhausted.

I want my body back.

I want the clear ejaculate which still trickles from my urethra when I come hard and fast. I want my clit back, the one the super surgeons, who can make almost anything into almost anything else, made by transplanting the very head, the glans, of my beautiful, long, ivory-pink-and-blue-veined penis right between my labia and then waiting three months for it to heal and the blood supply to stabilize, and then, in a second operation, carved down to the little clit-like apparatus I have now, which is somehow still so sensitive it makes me tense and shiver as the wife of the man with the cock hanging about two inches in front of my face uses her left hand to open my lips and her right to rub it inquiringly, watching my face closely for any reaction and then smiling in satisfaction when my eyes unfocus, my stomach muscles harden and my thighs spread a little of their own accord.

In your face, Joan, in your face.

In my mouth goes his prick, tasting at first of latex and then nonoxidyl-9, which makes my lips and tongue go bitter and numb. A little gag starting, and then he is in my mouth and firming up nicely, the glans beginning to extend itself along my tongue and pushing up against the

192

roof of my palate. An exciting and strange experience this, but stranger still is having had a cock, and having had women go down on it, I'm unwillingly, suddenly, almost shockingly aware of how each movement of my lips and tongue must feel to him. Strange, too, is that nerve endings which once made their home in my cock, and which now nestle in my cunt, are starting to remember too, and they're getting hot, turgid, and wet, and for several transcendent moments I cannot distinguish if I'm giving head to him, or to me.

He is fully erect now, much like my dildo, except the skin of his penis is very smooth, and gripping it with both hands, I feel an unexpected softness around a firm core. After a moment I begin turning on my hands and knees, moving around on the mattress to face his wife as we begin to kiss. Her black hair is loose and shoulder-length, her mouth is soft and wet and opens to hard little biting edges which nip at my mouth, tongue, and neck. I notice the small, downy hairs on her forearm, damp, and glistening in the overhead light. Her muscles work as she reaches for my cunt again, the hairs turning blonde as they catch the light.

Exorcising demons and ghosts. I told my closest friend I was 41 and knew nothing about men and didn't want to wake up at 51 and still know nothing, but the truth is much closer to the bone. The truth is that, unable to outrun or contain the contradictions of my life, I had been celibate for the past five years. I had dead-ended into every cold and silent secret I had trailed behind me into a dozen monogamous relationships and scores of one-night stands, but never once confronted. Until at last it dawned on me, lying in a bed I had entered only hours ago and would never see again, my hand cradling my chin as I watched the sunlight slowly traversing the coverlet, that all my adult life I had successfully avoided anyone butch enough to turn me on or top me.

And so your question brings me back here, Joan, to things I dream of alone at night, to desires I acknowledge in the dark, to exposed edges and hot, melting shame. To the things about which I neither speak nor write, to the things about which I truly care and therefore make a career of avoiding. "Your writing is very direct", you said, "you're very in-your-face."

I hadn't even known the word *transsexual,* nor that it was a word meant for me. In fact, I hadn't even known if transsexuals really existed, until at 28 I read Christine Jorgenson's book and finally admitted to being one. A year later, strung out, a suicide note wound in the typewriter and the garden hose snaked out to my vomit-green Datsun, I knew I would have surgery or have an end to it. I remember thinking I could always return to this place, but it would be a shame if a livable life was waiting on the other side of surgery with a patient, indulgent smile and I had not lived to see it. So I hauled my weary white ass into the Cleveland Clinic Hospital's Gender Identity Program.

But transwomen were supposed to be straight, and I had never looked twice at a man, nor felt any erotic heat in their presence. Determined to be a "successful transsexual," I worked earnestly at being straight, at developing the proper attraction to men. I examined their firm little butts, learning to decipher which were cute and which not. I cruised the hair on their chests, their beards, clothing and stance, the width of their shoulders and the bulge of their cocks, judging its length and thickness by the way it deformed the smooth, muscular profile of whichever jean-clad thigh it rested against. I faithfully reported each foray into heterosexuality to the hospital's noncommittal therapist, desperate to be the good patient upon whom she would confer surgery when my waiting time was up.

I finally informed her that I could not be straight, that I was a compete bust with men, that the only thing that still gave me my somewhat limp, estrogen-impaired erections, were other women. I knew then, suicidal as I was and living day-to-day only awaiting surgery, that when they threw me out I might make that trek out to the Datsun after all. "Oh yes", she said as she peered up from my chart, "we had one of those last year," and she went back to writing case notes in my chart about my "illness," and I went back to breathing.

This was pretty amazing stuff at the time. The head of the only other gender program in town had solemnly informed me I could not be a lesbian. "All transsexual women," he declared, "want to be penetrated." Well, yes. But I thought maybe he knew even less about woman-to-woman sex than I did, and fearing that his primitive sexual cosmology was accepted as revealed truth within the profession I hoped would save my life, I determined to keep my attraction to women as secret as my own pulse.

I learned, then, that I could be a transsexual and attracted to women as well. But could I be a lesbian? Certainly the lesbianism into which I came out in the '70s said I could not. It told me then, as it often does now, that I was a surgically altered male, a man invading women's space, my trespass tolerable to the precise extent I displayed the very oppressive,

195

stereotypically feminine behaviors from which many lesbians were in headlong flight. As for what lesbians did in bed, the women's community into which I emerged reversed the statement of the doctors: "No lesbian," it solemnly intoned, "wants to be penetrated." Penetration, I learned, was for straight girls.

A transsexual she-male freak and a lesbian slut turned on by penetration in an orifice still under construction was bad enough. Even worse, I found out that the type of lesbian I wanted meant I was "into roles." I say I was into roles, Joan, but in truth, it was all in my head. I learned from every quarter that roles were dead. Interred with them went the best of my desires: those strong, femmy butches who strode arrogantly across my dreams and scared me half to death with their power and my need.

Perhaps butch-femme roles *were* dead, though, for in truth I saw neither femmes nor their butches at the few women's bars or functions I was allowed to attend. Lesbians who professed support for roles were roundly ignored or actively reproached. The lesbianism into which I came out was dry and pale and bordered by bowl haircuts, no make-up, torn jeans, half-buttoned ubiquitous flannel shirts and humorless, hurting women whose sexuality was firmly suppressed, politically obedient, and completely foreign to my own erotic tides.

I didn't know butches and femmes still existed, Joan, or even if they ought to, until you started telling me about them. You taught me the theory, and even more you taught me respect, resuscitating the femme parts of me with words like *complex, courageous, many-layered,* and *specifically lesbian.* "For many years now," you wrote, "I have been trying to figure how to explain the special nature of butch-femme relationships to feminists and lesbian-feminists who consider butch-femme a reproduction of heterosexual models, and therefore dismiss lesbian communities of the past and of the present that assert this style." [1]

It was not until sometime later that you taught me the practice as well. And, moreover, that the women I craved still existed, that it was okay for me to want them, to imagine them. To picture their hands and cocks and hunger as I lay across my bed, eyes closed and back arched, rubbing the middle finger of my right hand across my own recently-made clit and pushing the new dildo I'd trimmed to just the right size and shape deep into my own improbable, impossible cunt.

"Oh, my darling, this play is real," you wrote in The Peristent Desire. "I do long to suck you, to take your courage into my mouth, both cunt, your flesh, and cock, your dream, deep into my mouth, and I do... She moans, moves, tries to watch, and cannot as the image overpowers her... and then she reaches down and slips the cock into me... I fall over her... I am pounding the bed, her arms, anything I can reach. How dare you do this to me, how dare you push me beyond my daily voice, my daily body, my daily fears. I am changing; we are dancing. We have broken through." [2]

I wondered, Joan, if I would ever break through, as I wandered through one night stands and short-time lovers, remembered the details of their bodies but not their faces, their technique but not their words. I actively avoided the type of women who excited me, turned aside their gaze, saw them in bars and left. Each time some hidden place inside me burned with a pain I forbade myself to touch or explore, desires and needs which are well-described by words like *many layered* and *complex*, but far more distressing and aching than the crisp, black letters on the flat white pages containing them.

The truth is, Joan, I had used sex but could not submit to it. I could come but I could not be present in my body, nor use it to express vulnerability or surrender. Sex was something I exchanged for safety or shelter or companionship. Sex was something to attract a lover who wasn't sure if she wanted a transwoman, and later sex was something to bind her to me through the shit she would take from friends. And, after it was over, sex was a way to be a child again for an hour, maybe two, in safe warm arms.

Sex was a way to humiliate myself and my lovers, to suppress and yet simultaneously revisit again and again those childhood nights when the humiliation was mine and mine alone, when the hot breath on my neck and back belonged to a complete stranger who only looked like my father and whom I met only in the dark. Every time I tried to make love, the image of my father hovered above whatever bed I was in like some kind of demented crucifix hung on the wall over our heads. The path I had trodden so long back to my sexuality, my body, and my lesbian self led in a beeline as long and straight and narrow as the lane-line down a flat-back Kansas highway right through to my father.

---

[1] Joan Nestle, "The Femme Question" in *The Persistent Desire: A Femme-Butch Reader*

[2] Joan Nestle, "My Woman Poppa, " Ibid.

Incest is a word too ugly and short to do justice to something which is much more than simply ugly, and too often not blessedly short. Incest is a daily thing, like the news, like dinner, like brushing your teeth. You can carry it around like a stick of gum in your pocket. It marks your body like a cancerous mole or a burn from hot cooking oil. It colors your thoughts like a drop of ink in a glass of water, and it poisons your life like shit down a well.

There are flavors and varieties of incest. There is the straightforward, no-nonsense kind that comes accompanied by clear, sharp snapshot memories developed by Polaroid. These are the ones you can take out and show your friends: who will commiserate; your therapist, who will analyze; and your family, who will deny. They are terrifying, but at least they have defined shapes, colors, and dimensions. Most significantly, at least they are known.

Then there are those as hard to grasp as smoke, the invasions and violations not captured on neat Kodachrome squares, lacking specific memories and penetrations. This is the kind I remember best. Just the glimpse and sense of probing fingers or too intimate caresses or special glances, and the adult passions of a parent too hot and close and hungry for a needy child to understand. The kind which, later in life, announces itself with only vague and confusing physical and emotional memories, welling up without warning or reason from unknown and uncharted underground springs, emerging from acts carried out at an age so tender there were no words to frame and recall them. Or perhaps a little older still, when words were at the ready and nearby, but quickly buried so well and far away they have no known latitude or longitude. Although they still manage to wake you from the dark in that familiar sweet sweat with your perpetrator's smell all over them, and your inner child-self screaming with fear and rage like a wounded banshee in close night air.

And there is another kind of incest, a kind no one even names. This is the transsexual kind, and it is a symphony of abuse. It is the Bach and Beethoven, the Haydn and Mozart of incest. It is orchestrated and complex, with woodwinds and strings, brass notes, and deep bass rhythms. It involves forcing female children to live as boys, withheld hormones and medical treatment, and quick, vicious punishment by those people you love and trust the most for the slightest omission or infraction in dress or behavior. Its terrors and confusions culminate in a second puberty in the full glare of midlife adulthood, followed by a gaudy, baroque crescendo of doctors and scalpels and stitches and blood which, however good the surgery, still leaves you feeling violated and broken inside somehow and never quite sane in your body.

And I am thinking of this, of your words and my life, as I feel his hands on me from behind now, warm and dry, rubbing gently on my buttocks, moving in widening circles until they pause and then dip between my legs, finding and then caressing the pink skin whose origins and construction I still cannot imagine. A single finger pauses at my cunt, stroking just inside my vagina and then tunnels slowly inward, so slowly that I cannot refrain from pushing back, surprising myself with a soft moan which sounds vaguely ridiculous, even to me. Even to me, who has walked the halls of this place many evenings, just listening to the sounds of women caught in the distress of their own lust, their overheated cries and whimpers clutching at my damp insides like a strong hand, or running clean through my body like an ice pick through warm butter.

His finger slides out of my pussy now, and I feel the first taut nudge of his cock. Holding it in his right hand, he searches patiently for my open, wondering vagina. After a year of work, my own dance is about to begin, Joan. You have helped to bring me here. I wonder: What will you think reading this? Will you be able to see the lesbian in me, in my experience? Have I come through so many rejections to face another? And, if you cannot read this, and read in it other lesbian lives and identities and appetites and passions, then who will? I have heard my own echo in your voice. Will you hear yours in mine?

Our lives become the enactment of those things we can think, the erotic acts and petty daily defiances of the fears haunting the borders of what we will confess to desiring, what we can imagine ourselves wanting to do with our own bodies and those of our lovers. The borders are drawn not by us, but by our fears, lines drawn in the sands of our need by rape or shame or abuse, imaginary lines in shifting sands we dare not cross. And standing on the other side of those lines are the women who have gone before, who have stepped past and returned to tell us what lies beyond, who can tell us about the parts of our lives we have lost, whose words we can read but not yet write, whose stories, at once terrifying and exciting, we carry around for years, running them over and over in our minds like old movie reels until at last we recognize them as our own, coming back to us like prodigal children returned in the night, or the echoes of our own voices thrown back at us from a cry of desire uttered so long ago, and in such pain, we neither recall it nor recognize its origins as our own.

He finds my vagina and, gripping my hips, he uses both of his wide hands to pull me back onto his cock. I feel my body parting to take him in, a familiar-strange feeling of pressure-pleasure as he enters me confidently, until at last he is in my flesh up to the hilt. I am struggling to take all of him now, and to stay connected as well: feeling him, testing myself, tightening obscure muscles far up inside my vagina. He pulls me back, the air forced from my lungs as if someone has struck lightly at my stomach, and just as I catch my breath he begins to move, accelerating now, the apex of his thrusts going off like some liquid explosion deep in the center of my pelvis. I am filled with a kind of wonder now, my body showing me things novel and unsuspected.

I close my eyes and collapse into his wife's waiting arms in slow motion. They know it is my first time, and she gently gathers me in, her hands cradling my face, pulling it down and in between her legs. I begin to lick her thighs, her groin, her clit, anything my hungry little mouth can reach, the sweet-smelling hair of her bush containing the sounds now coming from my throat. She laughs, a quick, easy sound, as I raise my hips to take more of her husband's cock inside me. Her plump, butter-smooth hips are tightly encircled, my arms gathering her whole cunt onto my mouth. I suck on it viciously, teething like an infant with bottle while another part of me concentrates on withstanding each delicious withdrawal and fresh, fierce entrance. I am in a kind of heaven, and for the first time in my life I am present in my body and unafraid. I am flying.

"We are the women who like to come, and come

hard," Amber Hollibaugh said. "I am a femme, not because I want a man, but because I want to feel a butch's weight on my back, and feel a butch moving inside my body." [3]

Nice as the maleness of my play partner is, it is neither female, nor what I want. I begin to play with my head a little, imagining he is a woman and his dick a dildo, strapped on with a soft butch's contradictory, perfectly masculine arrogance. Pleased and emboldened by the effect my magic lover is having, she uses her knees to lever my legs further apart. "Is it okay for you, honey?" she taunts, holding me like that for long seconds, pressing into me, pushing relentlessly forward and down, purposefully using her full weight so I need all my strength to support us both.

She leans far forward over the long muscles of my back, taking her time to pinch each of my nipples, and then pausing to wipe the small beads of sweat that have collected at my temples. "What's wrong, baby, is it too much for you?" she purrs. She pulls me backwards as she enters me so deeply; the O-ring of her strap is suddenly clear and cold on my butt. I catch a glimpse of her over my shoulder wearing the smile she flashes like a hidden blade, her teeth gleaming in the dim light with pleasure as my face contorts with that far-away look, as if I'd heard the whistle of a train, high-pitched and way off in the distance. Her free hand slips beneath me, trails along my belly, oblivious to my hips jerking sideways,

---

[3]See Amber Hollibaugh and Cherrie Moraga, "What We're Rollin' Around in Bed With: Sexual Silences in Feminism" in *Heresies 12: Sex Issue* (1981).

avoiding her, knowing her intent. She searches diligently for my clit, finds it, and begins to worry it, rubbing patiently from side to side with practiced, entirely successful fingers.

I am completely still now, holding my breath to deny her the reward of further response. Until something deep inside me just snaps, bursts clean, and groaning with rage and lust my back arches, a proverbial cat in heat, and she, laughing out loud, answers. Strong, veined hands grip my hips, and she makes the first, killing thrust that begins her final motion, and I know now that she will come fucking me, shouting hoarsely and thrusting into me just as hard as she is able. The warm honey butter-blood begins to flood the cradle of my cunt and I realize that for once my father is nowhere to be seen. No, nor my fear of masculinity and submission, of penetration and vulnerability, and closing my eyes to surrender to the first delicious tugs of orgasm, I know for the first time and with a certainty beyond simple trust that I am free.

(dedicated to the distant love of my life, the Head Femme, Ms. Joan Nestle)

Part III
From *Genderqueer: Voices from Beyond the Binary*

The Gender Cops

By Gina Reiss with Riki Wilchins

This is based on a story written by my partner Gina, who is one half of two (very) identical and (very) lesbian twin sisters. We reworked it together and published it as The Gender Cops.

The Gender Cops work overtime, form unions, walk beats. Gender Cops have big strong arms, hard hands, harder stares. Whatthefuckareyou? The Gender Cops make no arrests, just hand down sentences, to genderqueers like Fran and Robbi and me.

Fran's bangs, large hips, round breasts, my face. And Robbi's walk, part gunslinger, part runway, all boy-girl. My twin, my lover and me. And the Cops are out tonight, walking the beat, watching for crime. My twin, my lover, and me, we're on the run.

Fran has my face, gets the same stares, from the same men. She has the girl body, girl clothes. Dresses with long hair, soft eyes, pink pumps. I see her and see me/not me.

I'm the boy: boy clothes, boy body. Narrow hips, short hair, muscle-y arms. Shined loafers, navy tie, boxer shorts. We always have one mind, Fran and me, a twin thing. We're two equal halves of one full gender.

The Gender Cops hate us both. Hate Fran, and want to fuck her. Hate me, and want to fuck me up. They hate Robbi, because s/he's alive. Boy's clothes, girl body, post-op. A man with breasts shouldn't be allowed to live.

We keep on walking. The Gender Cops watch us pass. They weigh the odds, let us go. This time.

Another squad picks us up, on the very next street. Light turns green, we start to go.

Alex is my brother. Soft hair, cute smile. "There's no Santa," he tells Mom.

She has a friend call. "Ho ho ho," he says. "I'm Santa. You don't believe in me." Delighted, Alex scares him half to death.

"Been a good boy?" Santa asks. "Oh yes, Santa," Alex answers.

"What is your wish for Christmas," Santa asks.

"A hundred Barbie Dolls!" screams Alex at the phone.

Santa takes his time with that one. "Well, you be a good boy now.. Santa will see you at Christmas."

Next day Mom asks, "Who called?" Alex screams, "Santa called!"

"What'd you ask for? Momma asks.

"A hundred GI Joes," Alex answers.

True story. Alex knew. The Gender Cops are out. They work overtime, form unions, watch little boys.

We pass the next corner, turn left. One squad hands us off. Another picks us up, walks on patrol, stands at a post. The Gardens are in sight.

208

My other brother Peter hates soccer, plays with girls. At practice he starts to cry, leaves the field. Boys follow, calling names, making faces.

Mom reaches down, holds him close, wipes his face. Petey's tears leave long wet tracks, cross his cheeks, leave his chin. His face a window in the rain. I look through, seeing fear.

Mom looks at me: "I have to toughen him up," she says.

"Don't you dare," I say, then shout.

But no sound comes. My mouth won't work. Mom looks away. Pete looks at me.

Madison Garden. We round the corner. Go inside, find our seats. Settle in, then I get up.

"I gotta go," and then I'm off. I stand in line, ignore more stares.

I walk inside, and get yanked back. A large white woman, rosy cheeks, holds my collar.

"It says 'Women's Room'" she yells. I lift my shirt, and walk back in.

The Gender Cops work overtime, form unions, walk beats. Gender Cops carry large arms, hard hands, and harder stares. Whatthefuckareyou? Gender Cops make no arrests, just hand down sentences to queers like me.

A Continuous Nonverbal Communication

As I write this, it's been barely a month since the Word Trade Center attack. In the interim, we've been flooded with video images from around he world. Of all of them, perhaps none will stay with me longer than images of Afghan women, who inevitably appear on television as dark, human cocoons silently gliding across the screen.

It was telling that among the first acts of the new fundamentalist regime were demands that women cover themselves from head to toe and men wear full beards and masculine attire, and a reunderscoring of the illegality of homosexuality—all on threat of punishment or death. This instinct to control bodies, genders, and desires, may be as close as we have to a universal constant. It is common to culture rich and poor, left-wing and right-wing, Eastern and Western.

And here I mean *gender* in it widest sense—including sexual orientation, because I take it as self-evident that the mainspring of homophobia is gender: the notion that gay men are insufficiently masculine or lesbian women somehow inadequately feminine. And I include sex, because I take it as obvious that what animates sexism and misogyny is gender, and our

210

astonishing fear and loathing around issues of vulnerability or femininity.

In a society where femininity is feared and loathed, all women are genderqueer. In a culture where masculinity is defined by having sex with women and femininity by having sex with men, all gay people are genderqueer.

Fundamentalist regimes often begin with gender, because of all the things we have to say to each other, first and foremost among them is our gender. It's the reason we dress as we do every morning, style our hair in specific ways, stand and walk and gesture and even inflect our voices the way we do. Gender is what attracts us to other people and how we hope to make ourselves attractive to them. In fact, throughout our entire waking lives we are carrying on a continuous nonverbal dialogue with the world, saying, "This is who I am, this is how I feel about myself, this is how I want you to see *me*."

Unfortunately, when we do so, many of us lose our childhoods, our jobs, and even our lives, because in this continuous nonverbal conversation, the world is talking back to us too, saying, "No, no—this is how we see you, this is how you should feel about it, this is who you must be."

"The body," Simone de Beauvoir told us, "is a situation." She might have said a political situation, one that enmeshes us from infancy in a web of expectations, rules and demands concerning how we look, act, or dress, our sex and physical characteristics, what bodies we must desire and how we should desire them.

As we age, the web tightens. The gender transgressions of infancy are no longer as amusing or accepted in childhood; childhoods are increasingly unwelcome by the onset of puberty; and the gender experimentation of puberty must be abandoned by early adulthood when all young men and women are expected to be... men and women.

And only men and women. This ostensibly "natural" progression, inexorably producing men from males and women from females, consumes an extraordinary investment of social resources. Others devote time and energy to regulating our gender, and we spend an even greater amount learning, rehearsing, exploring, and perfecting our gender. By adulthood, our role is inhabited so completely that it feels inevitable. And should the experimentation of childhood inadvertently re-emerge, we find it awkward, embarrassing, and even threatening.

Threatening, but not departed. For although it looks like something we are, gender is always a *doing* rather than a being. In this sense, *all gender is drag*. And as with any drag, there's always the chance that we'll do something wrong, fall off the stage, do something unscripted outside the lines. So even a "real man"—all muscles, Clint Eastwood clenched teeth, and Sly Stallone dominance—might one day find himself crying during a movie, wondering what it feels like to wear a revealing dress, or feeling strange physical empathies with his pregnant wife.

In these moments of awkward embarrassment are also something like a kind of freedom, the hint of another kind of person we might have been, if only we didn't inhabit a world where every one of six billion human beings must fit themselves into one of only two genders.

This is a secret that the youth of today already know. Gender is the new frontier: the place to rebel, to create new individuality and uniqueness, to defy old, tired, outdated social norms and, yes, occasionally to drive their parents and sundry other authority figures crazy. More power to them. As one said to trans activist Dana Rivers, "I was too young for women's rights and gay rights. Gender is the civil rights movement of my time." Who could not be intrigued and stirred by such sentiments?

Yet the question still lingers: Why has it taken so long for gender's emergence as a civil rights issue?

Bang the Symbols Slowly

In the introduction to Sexual Politics, one of feminism's earliest manifestos, Kate Millett complained that analyzing patriarchy was so difficult because there was no alternative system to which it might be compared. Her comment could well apply to trying to analyze the gender system. The problem is not that we don't know the gender system well enough, but that we know it all too well and can't envision any alternative. Thus trying to understand gender sometimes feels like trying to take in the Empire State Building while standing only three inches away: It's at once so big, so overwhelming, and so close that we can't see it all at once or conceptualize it clearly.

Gender is like a lens through which we've not yet learned to see. Or, more accurately, like glasses worn from childhood through which we've always seen, and can't remember how the world looked without. And these glasses are thickly bifocal. They strangely show us only black and white in a Technicolor world, so that, as this book's narratives clearly illustrate, there may certainly be more than two genders, but two genders is all we've named, all we know, and all we'll see. And as basic as gender is personhood, changing that will take a more radical political upheaval than we've yet seen from any recent human rights movement.

Initiating such political action is made more challenging by the fact that gender is not only a formal system like marriage, backed by readily accessible public policy, law, and institutions, nor is it only a set of extralegal social practices such as are contained in the sexist treatment of women, or the racist codes of Jim Crow. Gender is primarily *a system of symbols and meanings—and the rules, privileges, and punishments pertaining to their use—for power and sexuality*: masculinity and femininity, strength and vulnerability, action and passivity, dominance and weakness. It's because gender is not just a system of laws and practices but also a way of thinking and seeing that it has taken so long to come to the fore as a political issue. Yet unlike the struggles against homophobia, racism, and sexism, the struggle against genderism will not only be about gaining rights for an oppressed class of men and women, it will be about gaining equality for all men and women. And, paradoxically, it will about the rights of some of us to not be men or women.

No Matter Where You Go, There You Are

As a system of meanings in which we participate each day, gender also feels exquisitely personal. So where someone gender-bashes or gender-baits us, we think *It's my own fault. If only I were more butch, if only I were more femme, if only I were taller, shorter, slimmer, heavier, had smaller breasts or larger muscles... if only I'd dressed or acted or felt differently, this never would have happened to me.* We blame ourselves, and so we try to change ourselves.

But feminism was right: The personal is political, and nowhere more so than with gender. The feelings of shame, humiliation, and fear are not the result of personal failings. Nor are they the inadvertent side effects of a benign system of gender norms. Such feelings are the gender system itself at work: enjoining us in policing ourselves, reminding us or our place, shaming us into submission, and making our gender appear natural, seamless, and voluntary.

Changing ourselves—becoming smaller, curvier, butcher, or thinner—will not change anything, because the gender system cannot be challenged or contested through individual effort. Genderism is an organizational and systemic oppression; it can be challenged only through an organized and systemic response.

If you come away from these writings with only one realization, I hope it will be that whatever feelings of shame or dread you've experience around your own gender are not just private problems, but political issues. And they are not yours alone, but something all of us have shared.

A movement for gender equality will not only have to work the halls of justice and the halls of Congress, but also engage with new and fuzzier sorts of political questions: How do we come to know our selves, how do we come to understand our bodies, and how have we come to be the 'us' that we are? It will need to begin thinking out loud about the political tools to recover that small inner voice that once said, 'This is who I am, this is how I see myself, this how I want you to see me.' A tall task for any new movement.

You're Trapped in Whose Body?

Another facet of the delay in gender's political emergence is that while cultural sensitivity to gender has exploded in recent years, it has also been strangely limited and stunted. All that explosive force has been channeled into one area: transgenderism. So whenever gender is mentioned, it is inevitably written down—and too often written off—as only transgender, something only affecting a small, if embattled, minority.

Oh, to be sure, we must all bow before the gods of inclusion. We must ensure no 'LGB' issues forth without it's trailing 'T.' But you and I, *we* don't have problems with our gender. All the men we know are tops, and all the women high-heeled femmes. While it's hard not to cheer the emergence of transgender as an important queer cause, confining the dialogue on gender to one identity has had the curious side effect of relieving the rest of society—gay and straight—from examining its own history of transcending gender norms.

But genderqueerness will not stay put in any one community. It's an issue that transcends boundaries and identities, if only because the boundaries and identities at issue are themselves gender-based. Rethinking gender will mean rethinking politics.

Gender originated as a feminist concern. Men were the norm and women considered 'the gendered sex.' Rather than attacking the binary, feminism emphasized redistributing power more equitably between the two sides. As gay rights grew, the gender dialogue centered on roles, as illustrated through the flamboyant dress and behavior of butches and femmes, tops and bottoms, queens and (later) kings. As gayness retreated to sexual orientation, a transgender voice began to be heard that was new, militant, and vocal, shifting the dialogue to more radical transgressions that involved changing bodies and sexes.

And now other voices are coming forward, promoting gender equality as a political movement and the next civil rights cause. Within these strands are all the tensions that have informed this book, and all the forces that have both delayed and promoted gender's emergence as a primary social issue.

This is a book for all of us. It's about the parts of us that have always been considered socially embarrassing, that every movement has left out and left behind because they were politically unacceptable, because they couldn't be 'mainstreamed' without changing that mainstream forever.

Well, the time for changing that mainstream is now. Gender is the civil rights movement our time, because gender rights are human rights. And I look forward to the day. when they are universally recognized and respected as such.

It's Your Gender, Stupid!

Gender. Everyone talks about it, but no one knows what it is or agrees on a definition. Gender *identity*? Gender *expression*? Gender *characteristics*? The gender *system*? A softer synonym for *sex*? Gender never stands alone, but always seems to need a noun to refer to.

It seems strange in a book devoted to gender that no writer takes the space to define what *gender* means. We assume that it's a common term of meaning, although it appears to be anything but. As with pornography, we may not be able to define it, but we know it when we see it.

The fact that *gender* is used in so many different but related contexts hints that we've touched on something very basic and pervasive in the human condition. So does the fact that we 'know it when we see it.' But I believe all the confusion surrounding gender means that perhaps just the opposite is the case: that gender is a set of meanings, and so, like children learning to tell Daddy from Mommy and little boys from little girls, we see it once we know it.

218

Early Morning Do

The most popular conception of gender is as a sort of inner substance, an essence we all carry within us, that is always conveniently binary and, except in the case of transsexuals, matched to our physical sex. It is the 'expression' of this gendered core that leads us to various gender behaviors, from wearing dresses or ties to displaying dominance or vulnerability during sex.

But according to theorist Judith Butler, gender refers not to something we *are* but to something we *do*, which, through extended repetition and because of the vigorous suppression of all exceptions, achieves the appearance of a kind of coherent psychic substance.

In this view, there is no doer behind the deed, no gendered identity behind the acts that we say result from it. The acts are all there is, and it is the strict regulation of these acts within the binary—females must produce feminine behaviors and males masculine—that produces the appearance of two coherent and universal genders.

Thus, I don't pull on certain clothes in the morning or style my hair a particular way because of something within me. I do these acts in a manner consistent with either masculine or feminine norms because to do otherwise would render me socially unintelligible. People wouldn't know what I was or how to treat me and I would be the target of a great deal of hostility. My achieving a consistent appearance and behavior is then offered as proof of a binary gender inside me.

If my gender is a "doing" that has to be redone each day, just like I put on those clothes each morning, that would help explain why sometimes my gender 'fails'. Even though I've felt like a man (and then later like a woman), people didn't always recognize me as such. Even I couldn't always recognize myself as such.

Better Dead Than Read

If I can 'fail' accidentally maybe there are ways I can fail on purpose that will create room for me to grow, to find new ways of expression that resonate more deeply. If gender is a doing and a reading of that doing, a call-and-response that must be continually done and redone, then it's also unstable, and there are ways I can disrupt it. Maybe universal and binary genders are not so inevitable after all.

This is an attractive line of thinking, especially for anyone who has found themselves transcending narrow, outdated, 20th century gender norms. Which is to say, all the writers in this book and most of its readers.

But how do we square this with some of the facts? For instance, transsexuality. It is undoubtedly true that some people (the author included) have, or do, feel a profound sense of discomfort at being confined to one sex and gender instead of another. If gender is a *doing*, does that imply that the transsexual in distress is somehow reenacting his or her own pain each morning in a repeated series of gendered acts?

And transsexuality aside, most people do report experiencing a stable, long-term sense of identification with either male or female, man or woman. That would seem to constitute pretty good evidence of gendered identities.

But then again, there are only two types of identities one can report experiencing. For instance, I said, 'I feel like a woman trapped in a man's body,' and my doctors understood and shipped me off to surgery. But if I'd worn my Intersex Society of North America, *HERMAPHRODITES WITH ATTITUDE* T-shirt and told them, "I feel like a herm trapped in a man's body," they wouldn't have understood and would have shipped me off to a rubber room.

Moreover, paradoxical as it sounds, there is room to question whether any identification, however stable and long-term, actually constitutes having an identity. Identification is always an act, a repetition, a name we give to a collection of discrete traits, behaviors, urges, and empathies.

A System of Meanings

Gender is a system of means and symbols—and the rules, privileges, and punishments pertaining to their use—for power and sexuality: masculinity and femininity, strength and vulnerability, action and passivity, dominance and weakness.

To gender something simply means investing it with one of two meanings. So anything and everything can be gendered, for example: ships, clothing, sexual positions, pens, bowls, hand positions, head tilts, vocal inflections, body hair, and different sports. Indeed, in many Romance languages every object is given a gender (*vive la difference, le monde, la dolce vita, el toro, el Riki*).

221

Because being gay itself is a transgression of the rules of gender, because those rules heavily disfavor femininity, gay and feminist (and lately transgendered) critics have tended to focus on gender's many repressive aspects.

The punishments we exact for using the 'wrong' words cross from the mundane to the fatal, including hostile stares in the women's room, being humiliated after gym class for being a 'sissy' or a 'dyke,' unfair termination for being a 'ball-buster,' assault for being a 'faggot,' arrest for 'impersonating a woman,' rape for being 'too sexy,' forced psychiatric treatment for gender identity disorder, genital mutilation for inter-sexed infants, and, of course, murder.

But, like any language, gender's primary effect is not repressive but productive: It produces meanings. These are created through a vast and visible top-down structure: binary birth certificates, restrooms, adoption policies, immigration laws, passports, and marriage laws. But notions of gender are also produced and maintained from the bottom up, through thousands of small, every day acts that create and destroy meaning in every moment. These micro-exchanges of meaning—in an elevator, over a meal, while buying a newspaper, even answering the phone—stamp us with our gender, bind us to it, and require us to answer to it in order to interact with other people.

Thus, not only does gender restrain us as individuals, but it is through the language of gender that we become who we are, that we come to recognize ourselves—and be recognized by others—as men and women, and only as men and women.

As an academic concept, gender has been

remarkably productive. Every year witnesses a new crop of articles, books, and theory about gender. Yet, as a civil rights cause, gender is just beginning.

One can see in a gender rights movement the outlines of something that links misogyny, homophobia, transphobia, and the restricted way we raise our youth. Indeed, a widespread understanding of gender rights would have enormous potential to transform society and remove inequity and violence.

A Sex By Any Other Name Would Still Smell as Sweet

If gender is a system of meanings, then what are we to make of the recent and remarkable degree to which 'gender' is replacing 'sex' to refer not only to men and women but also male and female? Perhaps this is only a way to avoid saying the overloaded word 'sex,' which also means intercourse.

It also seems to contradict the widely accepted notion that sex is a natural, physical property of bodies, while gender is something culturally derived from sex. In Butler's formulation, sex (male/female) is to 'raw' as gender (man/woman) is to 'cooked.' Sex is there 'on the far side of language,' while gender is something added on afterward.

The increasing use of gender to replace sex may be an acknowledgment, if only unconsciously, that once you start looking there is nothing, or at least very little, on the far side of language. As an experiment, I recently asked a large group of very hip queer youths to list on a blackboard all the attributes that made up a 'real man' and 'real woman.' Interestingly, on the list

223

beneath 'real man' was 'has a penis'; the list beneath 'real woman' included 'doesn't have a penis.' Not one person in the entire group thought to list 'doesn't have a vagina' or even 'has a vagina' as an identifying trait of bodies. I take from this that, although the body's moving parts may all be 'over there' on the far side of language, nearly everything we make of them to render them meaningful to us is right here, in our laps.

I'd Like to Buy a Women's Dictionary

Gender as a language is at once terribly simple, because it has only two meanings, and terribly complex, because it touches us across the entire plane of contact between our bodies and society. In most languages, words can be used by anyone who can master them. But gender is a language that creates and sustains binary difference. To achieve this, gendered signs must be highly regulated so they don't fall into the wrong hands, as if certain dictionary words were colored blue for boys and pink for girls. Wearing a skirt, smoking a pipe, crying in public, moaning during sex, scratching your crotch, describing anything (but God) as divine: These are some of the signs that may be given by only one half of the population or the other.

20/20 Hind-Cite

If gender is a system of meanings, then, in a book of the same name, what is meant by 'genderqueer'? For one thing, it brings back together those two things that have been wrongly separated: Gender and gayness.

For Butler, 'successful' genders are those that cite other earlier examples. Thus, we learn to become men and women and to be recognized as such by copying other examples. In popular thought, men and women are considered examples of 'real' genders, and drag, transsexuals, and butch/femme couples are considered copies. Thus, drag is to copy as woman is to real. Drag imitates life.

But if Butler is right, if gender is always an artifice that copies something else, then all gender is a reuse of familiar stereotypes according to the rules for their use. All gender is drag. And those that fail, that are read as 'queer,' are simply those that break the rules. Thus, neither a Streisand drag queen doing 'Barbra' nor Barbra herself doing 'woman' is any more or less real. There is no real gender to which they might be compared. Both use common symbols to achieve a visual meaning. The drag queen appears 'false' because we don't grant her access to those symbols.

Considering gender as a language, I would approach queerness somewhat differently. What did I mean when I told my doctors that I felt 'like a woman?' How was it possible for me to feel like anything other than myself? Perhaps I only meant that I was feminine. But, although one can be seen as feminine, feel feminine feeling, or to express femininity through our clothing, hairstyle, and posture, can anyone really *be* feminine?

Achieving femininity sounds like a lot of work: How I feel, how I express myself to others, and how they perceive me. It's one thing to feel consistently male, or feminine, or like a boy, but keeping all that feeling/expressing/being-perceived continuously intact must take a lot of concentration. Having any gender at all is really a sort of accomplishment, a sustained effort.

Genderqueers are people for whom some link in the feeling/expressing/being-perceived fails. For example, a stone butch may feel masculine and embody—in his own mind and behavior—masculinity. Yet, because of his sex (the pronoun strains here), she might still be read as womanly, like a girl trying on her boyfriend's clothes, especially if she is large-breasted and large-hipped.

If genderqueer bodies are those that fail because they don't follow the rules, the grammar of gender-as-language, then what are the boundaries of such a term, and what are its exclusions? Is a lesbian femme harassed for her miniskirt and fuck-me pumps genderqueer? Is a three year-old who tries on his sister's dress, or a 40-year-old who loses a promotion because her boss believes women should be seen-but-not-promoted? What about a football captain who's humiliated by his coach because he wept after a tough loss?

If genderqueerness is not something we do, but an identity we are, then none of these people would seem to be candidates. So one of the problems is that a narrow definition will exclude the millions of people who rub up against gender norms but don't step all the way out.

Some feminist theorists have questioned the queerness and radicalness of any sort of gender that doesn't do just that: leave norms behind. They consider transsexuals, butch/femmes, and drag queens as not only not genderqueer but actually gender-conforming, because they partake of binary stereotypes. For them the only 'radical' choice is adopting more androgynous genders that fall totally off the binary map.

But how are we to tell someone who faces discrimination or violence that they aren't really queer? Surely their attackers think they are.

Using queerness itself as a category of analysis seems to invite a new round of debate devoted to who is 'really queer.' A voice that originated from one set of margins begins to create its own marginalized voices. These twin problems of identities—boundaries and hierarchies—emerge whenever we truly try to base politics on identity.

It's Not Me, I'm Just on Loan

If gender is always a bending of self toward prevailing norms, then gender is always a kind of displacement, from which not even genderqueers are immune.

For instance, my friend Clare Howell recently said to me, 'I know I sound like a man.' This kind of displacement repositions her voice as coming from somewhere else. This is like the cross-dresser who declares, 'I like wearing *women's* clothes.' It's safe to say that no cross-dresser ever wore 'women's clothes.' If the bill came to him, they're his clothes, he bought them: They're obviously *men's clothes*. The displacement in naming them 'women's clothes' prevents us from getting outside the terms of the language, from getting to something new that might redefine skirts or dresses or femininity as being about men.

Many cross-dressers would reply that the point of dressing, for them, is that these are *women's* clothes. It is the otherness of the clothing, the fact that they are "women's," that is precisely what allows them to feel feminine. But once again, we can't get to someplace new, where femininity might be something about men that is not anchored in Woman (or vice versa).

(I remember telling my therapist one day in what felt like a breakthrough: If I'm a woman and I haven't had surgery, then this must be a woman's penis. Wet dreams must be part of women's experience. However, I would be slow to make this argument at the next feminist conference.)

I don't mean to fall into the familiar trap of criticizing those who want to eat their cake but not have it. Some genderqueers, including cross-dressers, are not interested in that 'something new.' They will always enjoy appropriation *as* appropriation for its own sake. These strategic displacements renounce ownership and participation. They announce that 'this part of my gender isn't me, it belongs to someone else, and I only appropriate/approximate it.' They announce an acceptance of a particular gender's rules of access, who 'owns' which words and who is allowed to use them. For instance, it's not possible for Clare to declare, 'I sound like other men with breasts' or 'I sound like other women trapped in male impersonators' bodies' or 'I sound like a Clare,' because those are not legitimate categories of description. By definition Clare must sound like something else, because her own body is not among the available choices.

Jenell, one of my favorite cross-dressers, always reminds me that hir enjoyment is transgression itself. If micro-miniskirts ever become fashionable for men, she'll have to decamp and find something else that is queer. In this sense, we are working somewhat at cross purposes. We both want to end the intolerable discrimination suffered by those who transcend gender stereotypes. But while I want to empty out those margins and bring queerness into the mainstream, he'd rather keep transgression in place, where s/he can enjoy it, but end its stigmatization. I think we both are right.

You Make Me Feel Like a Natural Woma (Impersonator)

Why do most genderqueers perceive themselves as falling within a long succession of binaries: female/male, butch/femme, top/bottom, boy/girl? Just as when we were children, we all learn to distinguish binary mommy from binary daddy, brother from sister, and little girls from little boys. It seems that like everyone else, genderqueers see in twos.

It is popular to explain genderqueerness as resulting from a 'spectrum of gender' along which all individuals—queer and nonqueer—fall. This is presented as a more enlightened and inclusive approach to bodies. Yet when you look closer, every spectrum turns out to be anchored by the same familiar two poles—male/female, man/woman, gay/straight. The rest of us are just strung out between them, like damp clothes drying on the line. The spectrum of gender turns out to be a spectrum of heterosexual norms, only slightly less oppressive, but not less binary than its predecessors. Maybe the problem is that gender is a way of seeing: black-and-white glasses through which we view a Technicolor world. Wherever we look, no matter what is 'out there,' we see only black and white.

There is an apocryphal story of an American anthropologist who visited a remote island where natives had 17 genders. Upon his return, he reported to the anthropological society that, "like all others we've studied, this culture also has only men and women."

We Are Men With Breasts—We Come in Peace

I recently spent a week at a large queer activist conference in the Midwest. I was dressed in my best Banana Republic menswear and looking, if I may say, pretty phat for a woman trapped in a six-foot male impersonator's body. I went across the street to a sports bar to get some change, and when I entered the whole room just seemed to stop: woman and men turned from the immense TV screen showing the Sunday NFL game to watch me. It was intimidating. I got suddenly very nervous and self-conscious. I knew, for these people, I might just as well have landed from Mars. Before I knew it I was raising my voice, feminizing my stance, and trying to blend in a little.

It's a hard thing to keep in mind when you're afraid, but I try to remind myself that if we can hold our course, it is at precisely such moments that we create a certain kind of freedom. At these times we are doing the best and the most anonymous kind of activism.

What, I always wonder, did those people see? I asked my lover on one such occasion what she thought people were seeing, and she replied, 'Well, you do look like a man with breasts.' Which, fortunately, was exactly the gender I was trying to do that day—as if that were possible. I only wish that option were available. Mostly I think people just try to figure out *what* in the world I am.

Don't Fuck With Mother Nature

There are lots of things about bodies and genders that don't fit the binary model into which we try to force them, even that most unassailable of binaries: biological sex. Biological sex is considered to be the most basic and natural product of bodies. All creatures reproduce, and to reproduce—unless you're an amoeba—requires two sexes. But consider the lowly seahorse, a creature that is said to "switch sexes" (no, not with the help of a little aquatic seahorse surgeon). We say it changes "from male to female" because what else could it change from or to?

The "female" hyena not only dominates its species like a male, but also has what any decent biologist would admit is a penis. Yet it must be a female, because it bears young. Or the male garter snake, which often morphs into a female after birth to attract male snakes to keep itself warm—something I might try during the next snowstorm.

What if reproduction doesn't have to include two sexes? Or what if there are other sexes, and they can reproduce as well? But that's not possible, is it? Because any creatures that can reproduce must be either male and female—*by definition*. Hence, surgeons' frantic search to locate the "real" sex of intersex infants before their genitals are cut up to resemble "normal" male or female. The infant's "real sex," *by definition*, cannot be intersex, cannot be whatever it is. Any sex but binary male or female is pathology, unnatural, and unreal, to be discarded and corrected with the knife. We say two sexes is "nature's way." But our male-dominated society has produced this feminine version of Mother Nature—

231

passive, pure, and reserved—when we need her, which then pushes her aside when the facts don't fit that perception..

The debate over the naturalness of binary sex is circular: Whatever reproduces must be one of two sexes, because there are only two sexes to be. Thus it is gender as a system of meaning that produces the "natural" Mother Nature, male and female sexes, and the gender binary that establishes what is genderqueer.

Queerer Bodies
When I Was in Gender and You Were the Main Drag

Somewhere inside yourself, you just know.
—nontrangendered lesbian explaining how she knows she's a woman

Inside, I just know.
—transgendered lesbian explaining how she knows she's a woman

Nothing in man—not even his body—is sufficiently stable to serve as the basis for self-recognition, or for understanding other men.
—Michel Foucault, presumably explaining how he doesn't know if he's a man or a woman, *Language, Counter-Memory, and Practice*, 1977

When it comes to gender, each of us, in our own private way, is an implicit philosopher. For instance, you probably believe that your body is male or female, that you are gay or straight (or bi), that feminism is distinct from gay rights, that physical sex is genetic but gender learned, and that sexual orientation is distinct from other kinds of gendered behavior. These beliefs probably feel to you like "just common sense."

But that is only because philosophical beliefs, aged in the keg, and widely enough accepted, are promoted to common sense. None of these concepts is just "out there." We think them because we think about bodies and the world in very particular ways. If you spoke about the thoughts a lot, people would call you a theorist, but if you spoke about really big thoughts, people could call you a big-amist!

Every model of bodies has margins where it begins to run out of explanatory steam, where we can see its assumptions, compromises, and limitations. And the people at those margins are those who bodies become targets for discrimination, because they transgress gender norms, because they are perceived as too old, young, Black, short, fat, disabled, deaf, hairy, ill, butch, flamboyant—or any of a thousand other things.

But it's not we who are broken; it's the model itself. It's the entire binary model of Western thought about bodies, sex, sexuality, and gender that is reaching its own limitaations, and everyone of us who stands outside or beyond it hastens the day of its demise. So I want to encourage you to think those big thoughts. Welcome to my breakdown.

'With a Capital P / And That Rhymes with T / And That Stands For...'

Bodies bear an enormous weight of cultural meaning. While acknowledging that bodies are 'really there,' one can reasonably question the meanings we give them. Anything but the barest facts—weight, mass, height—seems to go well beyond knowledge into the politics of meaning. I don't mean politics here with a capital P, as in civil rights and political parties. I mean 'small p' politics: the power to say and track and even control different things about bodies.

For instance, When I shaved my legs and put on my first dress everyone wondered what it meant. When I yearned for surgery, everyone thought it meant I was crazy. I thought it meant I really wanted to wear a dress and have a more feminine body. There wasn't anything else to know, any more than there was something to know about my inexhaustible craving for chocolate.

While my wearing dresses has resulted in my being diagnosed with a mental illness (gender identity disorder), it never occurred to anyone to ask whether my choco-craving constituted a mental disorder, because we don't regulate or politicize attraction to chocolate. If we did, no doubt, the nation's therapy couches would be filled with 'cross-chocolaters,' disgorging their deepest, darkest, semisweet secrets. ('And you were how old when *your mother* gave you your first piece of chocolate? Well! First, let's try something we call behavioral therapy. Just put your foot in this warm clamp here, hold on to this electrode while I plug in your chair, and we'll watch some *nice* pictures of chocolate together.')

Cashing in on Knowledge in a Different Register

Maybe that seems silly. But not as silly when you consider that, while our taste for specific foods passes without comment, our taste in specific bodies and pleasures seldom does. People immediately start asking what it means.

235

Why do men want to wear women's clothes? Why would a femme, who could have a 'real man,' instead want a wife-beater tank-top, strap-it-on butch? Why do some men want to become women? The only reason to track such things about bodies as their sex, genders, and desires is because we want to *do* something with them. Knowledge about bodies does not stand passively by, awaiting discovery by an objective and dispassionate Science.

Beyond measurable facts, knowledge about bodies is something we create. We go looking for it, and we fashion it in ways that respond to cultural needs and aims. We create the idea of binary genders because it marks something we want to track and control about bodies' appearance and behavior. We create gender identity disorders (GIDs) because we want to control sex and discourage the desire to change the body's sexual characteristics. We create the knowledge of sexual orientation and study it exhaustively because we want to know and control the individual's capacity to contribute to reproduction. There is no bright-line separation here between knowledge and politics. Knowledge marches to the beat of power. Specific kinds of knowledge *about* bodies enable us to exercise specific kinds of power *over* them. Such knowledge is not 'disinterested.' It is *very* interested, it is purposeful, it has aims.

For instance, when I went in for a nose job, the doctors were agreeable, quick, and friendly. But when I went in for that groin job, my whole life went to hell. Everything came under fire: my upbringing (probably failed), my mother (probably overbearing), my father (probably distant), and the demands of modern manhood (obviously threatening). I'm really a man (I'm still Arnold), finally a woman (but I look like Brooke), basically homo (news to my girlfriend), and actually a transvestite (news to my tailor).

Luckily for me, here come the professionals. Doctors, lawyers, psychiatrists on one hand and theorists, academics, and writers on the other.

The fact that many of us prefer different bodies, genders, or pleasures is clearly knowledge in the same register as the meaning of those bodies, genders and pleasures. In fact, I would go a step further. The propagation of norms for things like pleasure and gender, and the pursuit and categorization of divergence from such norms, are also knowledge in a different register. And the realm in which that knowledge lives is not Science but Politics.

If You're Not Part of the Problem, You're Not Part of the Solution

Prefer what is positive and multiple: difference over uniformity, flows over unities, mobile arrangements over system. Believe that what is productive is not sedentary but nomadic.
—Michel Foucault, *Language, Counter-Memory, and Practice*, 1977

There is a huge and ongoing current critique of Western knowledge—sometimes called post-modernism—that is questioning what we know, how we know it, and what effect it has on those on whom we know it. And of all the things we know, indeed feel we *must* know, none is more fundamental than our own

237

bodies. If that knowledge is showing cracks, then what else might be faulty as well? It is this nexus—the models of how we think and the problems posed by bodies that don't fit the model—that has led to the explosion of interest in genderqueerness and gender studies.

Whenever I wanted to feel feminine, I couldn't because I was a boy, too tall, too wide-shouldered, not 'real.' Later, when I sometimes wanted to fee masculine, I couldn't because I had breasts, I was too curvy, I was no longer a 'real' man. And when I wanted to feel something that was neither—well, that was impossible. It doesn't matter that some of these were things other people said about me and other things I said silently to myself. What matters is that the way in which we think—and especially the way we 'think the body'—has too often become an off-the-rack, one-size-fits-all approach. One that favors that which is universal, known, stable, and similar. But my experience of my body and my place in the world was exactly the opposite: mobile, private, small, often unique, and usually unknown. These are places familiar to many people on knowledge's margins, where many of us wish to go.

Truth Corrupts, Absolute Truth Corrupts Absolutely

'Let's assume you're right...'

'No, let's not assume I'm right. Let's assume there are lots of different rights out there and this is just one of them.'

—exchange in a gender seminar

The philosophical tradition, at least from Plato on, has always favored the concept of the same; i.e., the aim of philosophical thought has been to reveal the essential characteristics that two things hold in common.

—Newton Garver, *Wittgenstein and Derrida,* 1994

Why are we so frightened of difference and multiplicity? Perhaps it is the Western belief in the One True God? Strength, goodness, and truth are properties of our God's oneness. And all those tribes with multiple gods that monotheism considered , tribes that were slaughtered by the ancient Hebrews, must have been weak, false, evil, and duplicitous.

Probably we fear that the alternative to the universal is not plurality but an endless abyss, a chaos where no person's knowing is any more (or less) right than any other's. And if all this reminds you of the revolt against queer bodies as well as the 'threat' of multiculturalism, then go to the front of the class.

Some cultures accommodate, even exalt, difference. Yet in the West we pursue unity, we believe in singularity, we worship not only our God but final Truths. If it's not true somewhere, then it's not really true. There is no room for what is private or unique. To seek the Truth—always capital T—is to seek what is universal and perfect.

Unfortunately, such an approach is a kind of intellectual fascism that squeezes out individual truths. As the exchange quoted above illustrates, valuing of difference can cause real confusion in my presentations.

Good modernists that they are, my students

assume that there is a (single) right answer about things like gender and the meaning of bodies. Our job is arguing over the right one. It's a winner-take-all approach to knowledge. But where gender and meaning are concerned, there are lots of little truths. The way you understand your hips, your chest, your hair. How you feel when your lover holds you, gets on top, makes you come. The rush when you dress up, dress down, put on silk or leather. These are immensely small and private experiences. They are among our most intimate experience of ourselves in the world. And they are precisely what is lost when we propound and pursue singular and monolithic Truths about bodies, gender, and desire.

We have 'centered' all such knowledge over a binary of masculine/feminine. Body hair must mean masculine. Breasts must be feminine and passive. Hips are maternal, muscles masculine. An erect clitoris is vulnerable, an erect penis is commanding and strong. We need to de-center knowledge about the body. We need to allow other kinds of meanings to emerge, and other experiences of the body. We need room to find truths—always small t—that resonate with ourselves. To do this, many of us will need to transcend and transgress the kinds of knowledge that are out there. But that is how things change. That's why if you're not part of the problem, you're not part of the solution.

One Truth With No Trimmings, Please

Counseling, NOT Cutting! Get Your Scalpels Off Our Bodies!
—Hermaphrodites With Attitude poster

Knowledge is not made for understanding; it is made for cutting.
—Michel Foucault, *Language, Counter-Memory, and Practice*, 1977.

There is nothing abstract about the power that science and theories have to act materially and actually upon our bodies and our minds...
—Monique Wittig, *The Straight Mind*, 1992

If multiplicity is a pinging under the hood, a 'noise' in the system waiting to be found and fixed, then there's no louder *ping* than one that disrupts two perfect and complimentary opposite sexes. Male and female are Nature's way, our highest physical Truth. But what if Nature doesn't oblige? What if She exasperates us by producing bodies that aren't 'natural'? What if that pinging under the hood is the sound of genderqueer bodies that just... don't ... fit?

I am speaking, of course, of intersex infants. Such children, who are not clearly male or female, occur in about one in every 2,000 births. Because anything that is not male or female is not a true sex, we pronounce them 'abnormal,' fit them legally into male or female, and fit them physically into boy or girl by cutting them up at the rate of about five every day. Thus are 'natural' males and females maintained. In the aphorism of the Intersex Society's Cheryl Chase, intersex is the sex that can't exist. Because, by definition, every child must be male or female. Inside every intersex infant is a real boy or girl just waiting to come out.

For instance, in one segment of *Primetime*, a pediatrician showed color slides of intersex genitals

while Diane Sawyer tried to guess their 'real sex.'
That surreal exchange went something like this:

> *DS:* That's a male, right?
> *Doctor:* Nope. A female. And this one?
> *DS:* A female.
> *Doctor:* No. A male.
> *DS:* Now, this is surely a male. That looks like a penis.
> *Doctor:* Sorry, another female. This one?
> *DS:* Female.
> *Doctor:* Male.
> *DS:* Shee-it!

The surgeon's job is figuring out which sex the
child really is 'underneath,' whatever sex they
'appear,' and to surgically restore them to what Nature
intended. If Nature produces some kinds that aren't
'natural,' well, even Nature stops now and then to
down a brewski. Such doctors are not malicious or
destructive. In fact, they are anything but. They are
usually dedicated physicians and surgeons who are
doing what they see as compassionate surgery for
little, if any, fee.

But it is part of the peculiar tyranny of our taste
for perfect and singular Truths that difference cannot
be ignored but must be stamped out and made to fit the
model. If the model and the body disagree it is the
body that must give way. And this is the case whether
it's intersex infants, cross-dressing teens, or
genderqueer adults.

It's Always the Same Movie if You Don't Change "the Reals"

Part of the problem of applying notions of truth to the body is that lurking in the background is always the idea of what is real and authentic. Now, since I keep getting called 'sir' these days maybe I should create a whole new category called M-to-F-to-M, where I finally get to be Real:

You know you're a real M-to-F-to-M when...

* Your mother still calls you Richard.

* You tell your boss you're transsexual and he asks, 'Which way did you go?'

* You look at your girlfriend's naked butt and wish you had a good strap-on.

* Your lesbian girlfriend looks at your naked crotch and wishes you had a good strap-on.

We're back to different orders of knowledge here. What can it mean to say that my sister's femininity is real but that of a drag queen, a cross-dresser, an effeminate little boy, or an M-to-F is not? Why do we say that the masculinity of a Sly Stallone is real but that of an F-to-M, a stone butch, or a woman bodybuilder is not?

This kind of knowledge is still politics going in drag. It's about power. By creating notions of realness and dividing bodies along a binary of real/false, bodies like mine are kept disempowered. And, indeed, in places as diverse as my last job, the Michigan Womyn's Music Festival, my local women's events house in Miami, and the next women's room I have to use, I run smack up against the Real. Realness is not only about naturalness and the distinction between the groin you were born with and the one you bought yourself for Christmas. If gender is about language and meaning, then Realness is also about ownership, about who is allowed to use what meanings legitimately.

For instance, a drag queen is seen as appropriating women's symbols. No matter how convincing the illusion of femininity is, it's still an illusion because, by definition, the femininity is copied, not owned. The same is true for a transsexual. No matter how 'real' an M-to-F *looks*, she will never *be* Real.

Queer bodies are always defined by gender norms that are constructed in their absence. In fact, such norms are constructed only *by* their absence, because if they were there at the inception, the norm couldn't exist. It would be queered from the start.

It's particularly intriguing to hear charges of Realness coming from lesbians and feminists. Barely 100 years ago suffragettes were not considered to be 'real women' because they shunned passivity to invade men's social prerogatives. Only 40 years ago, lesbians were accused of not being 'real women' because they didn't want to marry men and become mothers. Twenty years ago femmes were ridiculed for not being 'real lesbians' because they looked like straight women—yet another kind of displacement that ceded femininity to heterosexuality.

And, of course, through it all, any man who slept with or desired the same sex gave up forever the hope of ever being a 'real man.' In fact, the United States may be the only country in the world where we are so insecure about gender that the words *man* and *woman* have no meaning unless they are preceded by *real*.

Realness circulates in so many different contexts because it is very politically effective. As a form of knowledge, it empowers some bodies, discourages others, and teaches all to stay within the lines.

Double Vision

'Can I ask you something—are you a man or a woman?
—attendee at women's conference

'Not always, but sometimes I think I am.'
—smart-ass author

What is it about binaries that so captivates our thinking: men/women, gay/straight, M-to-F/F-to-M, white/black, real/artificial, male/female, lesbian/feminist. Whoops... sorry. Scratch that. If there are more than two genders, it's a cinch that, with our bifocal glasses, we'll never see them. Actually, that's backward. Two-ness is not something 'out there' but a product of the way we see. We look for that two-ness. Our categories assure that we see it. That's why no matter what gender I do, the only question is 'Are you a man or a woman?' because that exhausts all the available possibilities.

When we pick up complex things—like desire or gender—with primitive mental tools like binaries, we loose nuance and multiplicity. Binaries don't give us much information. But then, they're not supposed to.

Quick: What is the meaning of masculinity? Mannish, not feminine, right? What about being straight? That means not being gay.

To say that I'm still really a man is only

meaningful in terms of my not being a woman. I am feminine only to the exact degree that I am... not masculine. I am gay only as much as I'm not straight, or to the exact number of songs I've memorized from *The Sound of Music*.

There's really not very much meaning or information circulating here, because with only two possibilities, meaning is confined to what something is not. As a form of thinking, binaries prevent other kinds of information from emerging. That is why no other genders ever appear. Binaries are the black hole of knowledge. Nothing is allowed to escape, so we get the same answers every time.

Two's a Crowd

In binaries all knowledge is broken down into two equal halves, right? Actually, no. Despite the name, binary thinking is not like two halves of an aspirin you break down the middle.

At this point in my life, I have spoken to hundreds of people about my body. Some of them even standing up. In 20 years, not one has asked me anything about 'gaining a vagina.' If they mentioned my surgery at all, every one said something, often in the form of a crude joke that was related to my losing the Magic Wand bit. Now, I'm as impressed with my genitals as the next person. Maybe more so. This is the same sort of question posed to F-to-Ms. It seems no matter what sex it is, it's about male.

It should surprise no one that binaries are about power, a form of doing politics through language. Binaries create the smallest possible hierarchy of one thing over another. They are not really about two things, but only one.

Consider Man. We understand Man as a given, universal, and inclusive. That's why we say 'all of Mankind' or 'the study of Man.' Woman is defined as what is left over: sex, procreation, and mystery. In this sense Woman is always 'Other.' Confined to what is not-man—sex, procreation, and mystery—Woman is always genderqueer. Asians are seen though the lens of Orientalism. What is Western and white is universal, while Asian as Other is confined to the mysterious, exotic, and primitive.

The second term of a binary exists only to support the first term. Thus, Woman functions not as an equal half, but as a support and prop, derivative from and dependent on Man. This gives the first term of any binary a lot of power. It defines the terms in which we talk. By doing so, it is itself insulated from discussion. We debate what Woman is, what women want, etc., etc. ad nauseam. But Man is immune from such debate. We endlessly debate the 'meaning' of blackness, but whiteness—until very recently—is a given.

Only by overturning binaries and binary thinking will we really be able to open up more room for the second terms to come into their own, for things now obscured at the margins to emerge. But toppling binaries is not easy. They are very compelling forms of thinking. For instance, I can promote genderqueerness all I want. But questioning whether 'real' sexes and genders—male and female, man and woman- really exist, just leaves me looking like a fool.

And as long as I can't question the existence of normative sexes and genders, it will be *my* body and my gender that are on the firing line, that I will be forced to define, defend, and write books about it, over and over again.

Genderqueerness may be a failed project from the outset. Our challenge is not promoting gender-queerness—as if it weren't already another way of promoting normative genders—but rather challenging the whole narrow, outdated notion of applying binary norms to bodies and genders.

See Through Transparency

In the beginning was the Word, and the Word was with God, and the Word was God... and the Word was made flesh...
—The Gospel According to John

In the beginning was Sex, and Binary sex was with God, and Binary Sex was from God... and Binary Sex was made flesh, and it was The One, True Thing about everyone's body.
—The Gospel According to Us

As a panel member at a gay journalists' conference, I wanted to talk about issues, politics, gender-based hate crimes and job discrimination. But first, audience members wanted to know what I 'was.' As reporters, they needed a label to identify me to their readers, not to mention their editors. The predictable questions flew. Did I consider myself transgendered? Was I presenting myself as male or female? Did I use male or female pronouns? Was I pre-op or post-op? Did I want to sleep with men or women (short menu in this restaurant)?

As I insisted on ignoring my personal life to focus on issues, their questions grew more insistent. The more I deflected them, The more demanding they became. Finally, several audience members became openly hostile, standing to verbally attack me with epithets and slurs, and finally physically assaulting me onstage with fist, chairs, and broken bottles.

No, wait a minute. I'm sorry. That was an S/M panel I was on. But, at the gay journalism conference, my audience *did* repeatedly question what I was, and express their frustration with my refusal to answer.

The question is whether language is transparent. Does it faithfully reveal the world, as though beneath a clear sheet of glass, or does it first create the world we say it reveals?

What kind of information did these journalists want?

Was I gay or straight?

Is it true I was transgender?

Had I had surgery?

I wonder what in the world these things had to do with creating gender equality for all Americans. Is there anything I could say about my body or identity to those journalists that wouldn't obscure everything I really wanted to tell them? Are there any names for myself I could have given them with which I did not completely disagree, which wouldn't have made me complicit in my own silencing?

Our belief in language is based on our naïve faith that the world is right here: finite, knowable, immediately and totally available to us. Thus, what isn't named doesn't exist. What is named must therefore exist.

I'll See it When I Believe It When You've Named It

Is the world really "right here?" Do words really describe the world accurately, exhausting what's "there?" Or are they limited only to what is repeatable and shared, and thus communicable? What about all those messy spaces between words and around their borders? Many of them are populated by our life's more profound experiences. Can language capture why you prefer wearing a nice dress to a new suit, why you want to penetrate instead of being penetrated, why you enjoy having a chest but don't want breasts, how you feel when you're stoned (not that the author has any experience here), or why you like Big Macs but hate sashimi?

Indeed, what about all those messy spaces between words like *feminine* and *masculine* and around the borders of words like *male* and *female* that are populated by bodies that don't fit the language? Or any of us whose gender experience confounds words when we transcend the narrow, outdated language of norms?

Words work well for things we can repeat, that we hold in common. What is unique or private is lost to language. But gender is a system of meanings that shapes our experience of bodies. Genderqueerness is by definition unique, private, and profoundly different. That's what makes it 'queer.' When we force all people to answer to a single language that excludes their experience of themselves in the world, we not only increase their pain and marginalization, we make them accomplices in their own erasure.

It is bad enough to render them silent, even worse

to make them speak a lie, worse yet if speaking the lie erases them.

All of us struggle with language used about them and against them: small, private experiences that we can never truly put into words. Our belief in language tells us that they aren't as real, as important, as the things we can say and share.

But I think it's just the opposite. For nowhere are we more ourselves than in those small, private moments when we transcend the common reality, when we experience ourselves in ways that cannot be said or understood or repeated. It is to those moments that we are called, and it is to those moments that we must listen.

Changing the Subject

My Mother Made Me a Lesbian (She Can Make One for You Too)

Sexuality 'did not appear until the beginning of the 19th century.' What had been some 300 years earlier just so many disparate urges, inclinations, and activities, we delineated as a problematic set of traits and drives that supposedly define a central aspect of human nature.
—John McGowan, *Postmodernism and Its Critics*, 1991

What do we mean by *identity*? No one is perfectly gay, completely straight, totally womanly, or wholly transgendered. So what do we mean when we identify as such? Are identities real properties of people, or are they more like approximations, normative ideals against which we measure ourselves but never perfectly fit?

What about those of us who are Democrats or over 50: why has sexual activity solidified into a social identity, but party affiliation has not? Why do we consider the Human Rights Campaign an identity-based group, but not the American Association of

Retired Persons? Is it perhaps because we politicize bodies' age differently than we do their sexuality?

Is gayness an essential property of gay bodies, so that when we look in the mirror each morning we see a gay person staring back? Or is it rather a way we learn to recognize and see ourselves in the mirrors of others' eyes?

Perhaps all identification is a kind of displacement, a loss of self that is replaced by a reference to something else that one is not. But if that's so, identity is not a natural fact of bodies—it has a history. It emerged through specific kinds of language and was a response to certain cultural needs.

Revolting Subjects

[I]t is already one of the prime effects of power that certain bodies, certain gestures, certain discourses, certain desires, come to be identified and constituted as individuals.

—Michel Foucault, 'Two Lectures,' from *Power/Knowledge: Selected Interviews and Other Writings,* 1980.

The 19th-century homosexual became a personage... The sodomite had been a temporary aberration; the homosexual was now a species.

—Michel Foucault, *The History of Sexuality, Part I,* 1978

According to Foucault, it was in the 19th century that the homosexual was created. He doesn't mean by this that same-sex attraction was invented on the spot.

253

On the contrary, for thousands of years people had known about disco, plaid shirts, show tunes, and whale watching, but sex was considered something one *did,* not something one *was.* Sex was an appetite, just like our appetite for food or money. If you liked one things and not another, that was a matter of personal taste. People were still considered to have sexual problems, but not the way we think of them. If you used sex for humiliation or conquest, if you pursued it to excess or pined away in lust, then, yes, you had a problem with sex. But the problem was how sex was used, not its direction.

But in the 1800s, scientists produced a new catalog of diseases based on sex. It included: gerontophiles (old people turn you on), pedophiles (young people turn you on), onanophiles (you turn you on), zoophiles (horsies turn you on), masochists (a little pain won't hurt), sadists (especially if it's someone else's), necrophiles (don't ask), and of course the homosexual (don't tell). Such people were thought to be joined by shared emotional traits, physical dispositions, latent characteristics, childhood experiences, family histories, and so on.

A new kind of knowledge had been created, and along with it a new category of self-experience. It now became possible to experience one's self *as a homosexual* and to be identified by others the same way. And now we have a powerful civil rights movement based on this self-perception invented just 150 years ago.

As sex went, so did gender. Diseases like 'transvestic fetishism' and 'gender dysphoria' were added to the catalog. Individuals who transcend gender norms have been around since the first culture created norms and then tried to impose them. But we are now witnessing the emergence of a whole new class of people, once simply 'queer,' who now understand themselves *as transgendered individuals*, although the word did not exist 10 years ago.

FertilityQueers: Voices From Beyond the Sexual Binary

Two concerns: is this really a big change in people's thinking? If so, how are such powerful effects achieved?

To the first concern, it's easy to respond that the idea of the 'invention' of the homosexual is just 'playing semantics.' It may or may not be semantics, but it is not any sort of 'play': the effects of such forms of knowledge are both profound an personal.

Quick: what is the name for the identity we use to refer to infertile women? How about women who have XXY chromosomes? Women who are masculinized because they produce too much testosterone? Mothers who like wearing suits and ties to work?

There are no such identities, because these are not bodies we want to track and control. But women who've had sex changes? We *all* know the name created to track *that* identity. But suppose, as with these other bodies, we didn't care about a woman's surgical history? Then such individuals would simply by "women," and the whole discourse around transgender and the politicization of such bodies would not have happened, as it did not with these other kinds of women. Yet there is no doubt, had we given them an identity, categorized them socially and legally as not being "real women" and subjected them to widespread discrimination and violence, we would now be witnessing the emergence of a community of such individuals, and a political movement to represent them, along with their demands for inclusion within feminist (and lesbian) organizations and books like this one to promote their visibility.

How to Be Hip

Nor are the effects of such forms of knowledge confined to the political sphere. For instance, when I first decide to change my body, I was told I was transsexual. I just wanted to change my body, but I was told the reason for this was that I was a 'woman trapped in a man's body.' I had a gender identity disorder. So I learned to think of myself as having a 'birth defect,' characterized by my new mental disorder.

When I entered the lesbian-feminist community of Cleveland Heights, Ohio, I was told I was still 'really a man' or a 'surgically altered she-male,' in short, some kind of gender freak. I was kicked out of my apartment, shunned in bars, and barred from local events. Painful as this was, even worse was my buying into what was being said about me. I learned to think of myself as some sort of man-woman, neither male nor female: not even appropriate for my (lesbian) lover.

With the advent of transgenderism, I finally had a way of thinking of myself that gave me a sense of pride. I began to understand myself as transgendered. And, of course, at some point, that didn't work either, because like everything that preceded it, it didn't really fit.

It's not that I'm especially impressionable. To understand our bodies at all we must make a stand somewhere. There is no neutral place; no position outside of language. We seek ways to understand our bodies that solve what we perceive to be their problems.

In my case, the problem that what was created about my body was its genderqueerness. I sought ways of understanding it that would resolve that problem: some painful, some empowering. The problem could have been many other things. For instance, there's the gentlewoman who sat next to me on the bus, saying, 'Please excuse my fat hips.' When I asked her about his, she said, "I know! My feminist friends said I should think of them as nurturing and maternal." We had a long talk about her hips and my body, and how miserable they'd made each of us.

Was she especially susceptible? I doubt it. But someone had explained to her that her hips were "width-queer," and that they transcended some norm somewhere. She had internalized this as a problem of her body, and sought ways of understanding it, just as I had, that would explain its "meaning."

Indeed, two things stand out most about our stories. First is how feminism's counter-discourse on women's bodies has, in its own way, become as narrow and inflexible as the one from which it was supposed to free us. Second is how much the understanding of our bodies has colored how we feel about them. I doubt my wanting to change my body, or that woman, her hips, had much implicit meaning. But the attachment of meaning is a powerful tool for making us experience ourselves in the world in very specific ways.

You Cut Me Up

Which brings me to my second concern: how are such effects achieved? As good progressives, when we think of Power, we imagine something above us, overwhelming and harsh, that we need laws to rein in. This works well with big, institutional power, like the police powers of arrest, the power of courts, and the government's power to spy on us or restrict our speech. But that kind of power doesn't go very far in explaining that woman's hips or my body. After all, there was no central registry tracing us, and no governmental agency compelling our experiences.

For that kind of power, we need another model: discourse. I seldom use the word, because when I do, Clare thrusts two fingers down her throat and makes gagging sounds. Academics may overuse it, but I think it's useful here. Discourse simply refers to power "from the bottom up." This is the kind of small power exercised in hundreds of little everyday transactions.

Think of the body's surface as a sheet of cookie dough. Because the dough has no inherent meaning, you can cut it all into circles, stars, or squares, or a mixture of different shapes all at once. When you're done, no doubt the cookies are 'real.' But there is no 'truth' behind them, nothing to be learned from why one is a star and not a triangle, and no shape was any more *there* beforehand than any other. What truths there are lie with the cutter, not its product. Discourse is the cookie cutter.

But, wait. All this is too abstract. Why don't you take a break for a minute, go down to the corner newsstand and buy a *Times*?

News to Me

Fine. Does the man ahead of you hold the door for you as you leave your building? Do people step aside when you walk down the crowded street, or do they unconsciously expect you to step aside?

When you get to the newsstand, does the newspaper vendor address you as 'Sir,' 'Ma'am,' or 'Miss'? Perhaps he finds you sexually confusing and stumbles awkwardly over pronouns. When he hands you your change, does he look down in respect, meet your eyes, or perhaps refuse to acknowledge you at all? Does he smile in friendliness or frown in disgust? If he's the guy you always see, before you leave, does he swap a dirty joke or ask about 'the wife and kids?' Or maybe he flirts just a little, asking if you've lost weight and telling you that you need a young man in your life?

Even in this tiny exchange, a small fraction of your day, one interaction after another is piled up that stamps us with our sex, gender, or class. This is not power from the 'top down,' but from the 'bottom up.' It is not the big, familiar power of concrete buildings and visible institutions, power that is both massed and massive. Rather, it's the power of what is said and thought about us: the small, diffuse, invisible power created and instantly destroyed in thousands of little, insignificant exchanges.

It is through just such interactions that fat hips and queer bodies are made, interactions that tell us what we are, what we mean, and to what names we must answer.

Help! Youth Are Escaping the Stable!

If this power of discourse is created and destroyed over and over again, then it must be inherently unstable, too. What happen if it "fails"?

What about the homosexual? Could some people who are gay simply fail to acknowledge it? Not going into the closet, but simply refusing to answer to the name?

That is exactly what is happening among queer youth. As we've seen, identities are created in response to the politicization of bodies and desires. Eventually a countermovement emerges—as it did with homosexuals and now is doing with gender—to fight that politicization. But as this countermovement becomes successful, a paradox ensues. The more successful it is, the more unstable the discourse becomes. Gays show up on TV, in movies, as politicians running for office: gayness is no longer so "queer."

Sexual orientation becomes less of a problem. Young gays and lesbians don't walk down the street holding hands like we did, terrified, self-conscious, and staring rigidly straight ahead. They just walk around holding hands openly like their straight classmates. As the oppression that defined gay identity shifts, so does the meaning of the identification. Young queers face new possibilities, they can be other kinds of individuals, they can explore other selves.

Luckily for us, one of the selves many have used their new freedom to explore is gendered. Increasingly, numbers of youth are asking, 'If I don't have to be gay anymore, what other selves are there

260

for me to explore? Who might I be in another gender?' Gender, the old battleground, is quickly emerging as the new battleground, and the new playground, for today's youth.

Put Down That Clipboard or I'll Shoot

The ways in which we formulate notions of selfhood out of the models of subjectivity available to us, shape our behavior in the world.
—Patricia Waugh, 'Modernism, Postmodernism, Feminism: gender and Autonomy Theory,' from *Postmodernism: A Reader*, 1992

Do not demand of politics that it restore the 'rights' of the individual, as philosophy has defined them. The individual is the product of power.
—Michel Foucault, *The History of Sexuality, Part I*, 1978

We are used to taking the side of individual rights against institutional and governmental power. And we have centuries of political thought and experience to guide us in such struggles. But as Nancy Fraser notes, 'Talk of rights and the inviolability of the person is of no use when the enemy is not the despot but the psychiatric social worker' with a clipboard. (Nancy Fraser, *Unruly Practices: Power, Discourse and Gender in Contemporary Social Theory*, 1989, p. 44)

With discourse, we're thinking about a completely different kind of power—one that creates individuals. Our old political and theoretical tools don't apply. If the homosexual and the transgendered are themselves the product of certain kinds of power, we need new kinds of political action that will call into question individuality itself. Our problem is not fighting for the rights *of* specific individuals, but rather fighting for the right to *be* different kinds of individuals.

In other words, the question for genderqueers is, do we want to fights *as genderqueers*? Or do we want to question the whole project of queerness? Do we want to make genderqueerness OK, just as gay rights is making gayness OK? Or do we want to attack the notion of normative genders itself?

The question is not as trivial as it sounds. For instance, a transgender movement devoted mostly to the problems faced by transsexuals has the capacity to help a lot of embattled people. Yet it will leave out many people who are often genderqueered but not trans.

Do we want a transgender struggle that focuses on the rights of transsexuals to change their driver's licenses, get surgery, and transition on the job? Or do we want a movement against the gender stereotypes that affect all Americans? This is not a rhetorical question. As gay rights continues to mature, the fight for gender equality looms as the next major civil rights struggle on the horizon. Our answers to such questions will have enormous power to shape what comes of it.

Deconstructing Trans
We're Just Like You, We're Just... Different

When a lesbian—perplexed at the furor over trans inclusion in her organization—asked me, 'Where were transpeople 20 years ago?' I told her, 'They were there, but they were gay.'

I wasn't being snippy, but accurate. In the '70s they *were* there, and they *were* gay. But, in just 20 years, they were neither.

Gender should have been the quintessential issue for both gay rights and feminism. And both owed a substantial debt to genderqueers: from outspoken suffragettes to radical dykes; from the genderqueers who rioted at the Stonewall Inn, to nelly boys picked out for assault.

But in the late 1970s and the '80s, both the gay and feminist movements turned away from gender as a primary issue, both for social and political reasons. The political reason was that following the success of black civil rights, minority rights turned definitively away from freedom of expression in favor of 'immutable characteristics': things you can't change even if you want to.

If there's something socially undesirable about

you that you *won't* suppress, then it's a matter of choice and not the law's concern. But if it's something undesirable that you *can't* suppress (race, disability, ethnicity), then the law should offer you protection. This has shortchanged the right to self-expression. It has made social legitimacy an effect of helplessness before your own sexual and gender orientation and whatever biological foundation you can put forth to explain them.

In the gay community the focus on immutability has led to promoting sexual orientation in a way that is completely removed from gender expression. Gay men never act effeminate, don't ear pastels, don't brandish limp writs, and wouldn't be caught dead lip-synching to Barbra Streisand's Broadway album. Lesbians aren't butch, don't ride motorcycles, never sport crew cuts, and only wear combat boots if they've just come from Army boot camp.

In the trans community, just the opposite is the case. Gender is promoted at the expense of sexual practice. It's OK for me to say I'm changing my body because of my 'gender identity.' But it would considered superficial, even perverse, to say I was doing so because having a more feminine body would turn me on. Among cross-dressers, it's acceptable to say that I wear women's clothing to 'explore my feminine side,' but not because it gives me an erection.

That's the political, but there's also the social reason these movements turned away from gender. Looking gender normative is vital to social acceptance. That's why few things are more uncomfortable than seeing someone whose gender you can't discern, or more socially unacceptable than being a man who looks and acts like a woman, or a woman who looks and acts like a man.

When gay activists began asserting, "We're just like straights, we just sleep with the same sex," that "just like" was shorthand for "gender." It said, "We look and act just like your parents, your friends, or your boss: don't be uncomfortable with us."

And when feminists began explaining, "We're not trying to be men," the phrase "trying to be men" was also shorthand for "gender." It said, "We're just like your wives, mothers, daughters: don't be uncomfortable with us either."

While the intervening years have proven this to be very successful rhetoric, they've also proven that it isolated genderqueerness as a civil rights issue. That was the price of social acceptance for two new and often-threatening movements.

It's fair to say that "transgender" was created by the gay and feminist movements. Its emergence became practically inevitable from the day those movements began moving away from gender.

A Hard Man is Good to Find (But That Has *Nothing* to Do With My Gender)

Most remarkable in gender's evolution as an issue has been the widely accepted separation of gender and sexual orientation, even among transgender activists. But is desire really distinct from gender? Only if we confine *gender identity*, as many gay organizations have done.

Watch any butch with big biceps, tight jeans, and a lit hand-rolled cig walk into the local gay bar. Or a butch queen at the gym spending hour upon hour pumping and primping so he's buff enough to catch the eye of that cute new number with the tight butt, long eyelashes, and rippled abs. Or watch them in bed, one raising his butt, spreading his legs, and moaning to arouse the other. It is only through such gendered behaviors that sexual orientation is consummated, that it makes any conceptual sense. These behaviors are how we make ourselves attractive to others, are attracted to them, and make love.

Moreover, sexual orientation will always be tied to genderqueerness, because desire *itself* is gendered. A man having sex with a man or a woman having sex with a woman is itself the most profound transgression of gender norms conceivable. It is at the heart of homophobia.

It need not harm gay political aspirations to admit the obvious: that if it is gender-feminine to pull a dress over the male body, it is gender-feminine to pull a man down on it as well.

The Queerer Sex

Where is feminism in this today? Why has transgenderism remained the source of long-running tensions within feminist ranks? Genderqueerness would seem to be a natural avenue for feminism to contest. Woman's equation with nurturance, femininity, and reproduction—in short, to trouble the Project of Man, the ideal of two binary, eternal, separate-but-equal sexes. Yet feminists have been loath to take that avenue, in no small part because queering Woman threatens the very category on which feminism depends.

Man is the universal. Woman is defined by her opposition to Man, by what she does not have, the Penis, and the one thing she has that Man does not: reproduction and sexuality. Thus, to be androgynous is not gender-neutral, but male. Man is the default sex; womanhood must continually prove itself by artifice, adornment, and display. In a culture centered on Man, Woman will always be the genderqueer. This has made Woman an inherently fragile project. Feminist and lesbian communities have remained deeply unreceptive to the new barbarians at the gate—F-to-Ms, M-to-Fs, passing women, cross-dressers, drag kings and queens, and tranz youth—who seem to threaten the very foundation of Woman, while male communities feel no such concern. A bearded, muscle-bound F-to-M evokes nothing like the same resentment, anxiety, and concern for authenticity in a men's group that either he or an attractive, curvaceous M-to-F does in a women's group.

It may take a new generation of young women to take queerness to its natural feminist conclusions— women for whom such queerness is not a threat but a new kind of feminist freedom.

Only Half the Man I Used to Be

"Transgender" origins lie in the search for a name for people who didn't want to change sexes (as transsexuals do), or who occasionally change to clothing of another sex (as cross-dressers to), but who wanted to change their genders: live full-time in another sex without medical intervention. Over time, transgender came to be used for anyone who

267

"transgressed gender," including—according to who you ask—cross-dressers, transsexuals, and the original transgendered but also butch women, effeminate men, intersexuals, drag people, and genderqueer youths.

The term has not been without its conceptual awkwardness. Defining a class of people by "transgressing" norms would seem in some way to reinforce those norms. In addition, it defines people by what they are not—normal men and women. However, *transgender* has undoubtedly enabled many despised and marginalized people to come together around a common voice, and a way to identify that is empowering and constructive.

Most cities now boast a local transgender group, and today, transgender conferences are being held somewhere in the United States almost every month. There is even a kind of tenuous artistic legitimacy, as transsexuals find their way into movies like *Boys Don't Cry* and *Hedwig and the Angry Inch*. With this legitimacy has come political activism: transsexual activists now pass local ordinances, educate policy makers, and win lawsuits. And while transgender's increasing acceptance has not stopped the flow of blood from trans murders and hate crimes, there is reason to hope.

Let Me Hold That Umbrella for You

Transgender was intended as an umbrella term— a name for inclusion. But umbrellas don't work well when one group holds them up. Today, trans activism is often focused on the problems (bathroom access, name change, workplace transition, and hate crimes) faced by those who have been most active in its success: postoperative transwomen (any similarity to the author is purely coincidental).

Yet there is little being done today to address the needs of drag people, butches, cross-dressers, transsexuals who do not seek surgery, or (besides the Intersex Society of North America) intersexuals. Cross-dressers especially have suffered from a lack of representation, although they number in the millions, and experience severe problems associated with child custody, job discrimination, have crimes, and punitive divorce precedents.

Thus has transgender, a voice that originated from the margins, begun to produce its own marginalized voices, and in part because it is an identity organized around "transgression," there is a growing debate over who is "most transgressive."

In Surgery We Trust

How does one decide such questions? For instance, as one transsexual put it, "I'm not this part-time. I can't hang my body in the closet and pass on Monday."

There is no doubt, from one perspective, that cross-dressers enjoy some advantages. They are large in numbers, most only dress occasionally, and they can do so in the privacy of their own homes. Does that mean they would live that way if they had a choice? Does it really make them "less transgressive"?

In fact, nobody wants men in dresses. There are no "out" cross-dressers, and almost no political organization wants them or wants to speak in their name. "A man in a dress" is the original "absurd result" that judges, juries, even legislators try to avoid at all costs when rendering verdicts or crafting laws. "Men in dresses" isn't the next hit movie; it's a punch line in the next joke.

Among genderqueer youth, it is no longer rare to hear complaints of being frozen out of transgender groups because they don't want to change their bodies. In an identity that favors transsexuals, changing one's body has become a litmus test for transgression. And even that litmus test is not always applied.

For example, one would assume that preoperative transsexuals (or the increasing number of nonoperative transpeople) would be considered more transgressive, as would transgendered people of any stripe who don't "pass" as binary males and females. A 6-foot, 3-inch pre-surgical transwoman with a deep voice and five o'clock shadow is doing the hardest, loneliest, and most dangerous gender activism there is. The same could be said for a 5-foot, 2-inch butch with a pear shape, small hands, and high voice who insists on having her masculinity recognized, acknowledged, and respected.

Yet these are not the individuals who are highly prized as 'most transgressive.' In fact, as with most communities founded on oppression, the opposite occurs: those who can pass are most highly valued, as are those whose surgery makes them legally male or female. Since trans activists have loudly and justifiably complained about being "most transgressive" and about being consigned to the bottom rung of gay and feminist concerns, so it is doubly unfortunate to see them developing hierarchies of their own in which transpeople must compete for legitimacy, and in which their own margins sometimes go unrecognized. Indeed, like assertions over who has more "privilege," debates over who is most "transgressive" are a form of reverse discrimination that seeks to confer status based on who has it worst.

Which is to say, debates over identity are always divisive and never conclusive. They are divisive because at heart they are about conferring status, always a zero-sum game. For one person to win, another must lose. They are inconclusive because there are no objective criteria by which to decide. Winning such debates is always a function of who set the rules and who gets to judge. And since post-surgical transsexuals are most often in a position to judge, at the moment, the rules tend to favor their life experiences.

You're Indescribable

Transgender is now commonly used in two ways: as both an identity and a descriptive adjective. As an identity, it faces the same question as gender itself. Is it transgression about something we *are* or something we *do*? So far the answer has been definitely 'something we are.' This has created an interesting collision between theorists who understand gender as a *doing* and many transsexual activists who assert it as a *being*. Put another way, the theoretical arguments being used to promote the importance of transsexuality risk undercutting the political arguments those same transpeople are using to advance their political legitimacy.

Organizations seeking to add transgender issues to their work add "gender identity" to their mission statements—a psychiatric term (from "Gender Identity

271

Disorders") related to transsexuals. But when we equate transgenderism with those individuals who can claim *their* gender is a sign of an internal, binary essence, we privilege transsexuals over other genderqueers who cannot make similar claims. Moreover, we diminish those who conceptualize their transcending of narrow gender stereotypes as a matter of the right to self-expression.

If a boy is repeatedly beaten up after school for being a "sissy," can he plausibly claim that his "sissyness" results from some inner identity? What about a big-breasted femme who is sexually assaulted for being perceived as "sexually provocative"? Does the fact that they cannot claim their transgression to result from a "gendered identity" make it any less meaningful? Some gay and trans activists would reply, "Yes."

While transgender was promoted as including butches, femmes, and drag people, it is hardly univeral among them, and for the most part it remains firmly anchored in the experiences and political desires of transsesxuals. Perhaps one lesson is that when an identity cannot be applied equally, those who are less equal refuse identification.

And while there are undoubtedly millions of Americans who frequently transcend gender roles— from ballet-loving quarterbacks to suitcoat-wearing soccer moms—the identity remains inhospitable to them as well.

Too Queer for Words

Some trans activists have tried to correct these limitation by "embracing the contradiction." They emphasize the big-tent approach of transgender-as-adjective, and assert, "We are *all* transgendered." This rings true, but does it also ring useful?

If people refuse a term as identity, is it more likely they will accept it as a description? If not, of what use is describing people with an adjective they reject? The emphasis on transgender as a description also harks back to the idea of *all* gender as drag, as a kind of displacement of self into binary norms. Yet many transsexuals reject such arguments. They understand—and want others to understand—that their gender results from a core identity, a true self that is not the result of some external norms.

Moreover, many transgender people are attracted to the term because it is not openly inclusive, because it *does* name a specific group of people . They accept *transgender's* wider use when it leads to greater social acceptance. But they would deeply resist the guy in the next cubicle who wept over last night's Super Bowl loss to the Packers, saying "Yeah, I cried. I guess I am transgendered."

In fact, GenderPAC's reaffirmation, in 2000, of its mission to be a human rights group for all Americans, drew angry rejoinders from many trans activists who wanted a gender rights group that was exclusive to them. Among the loudest voices were those who had been calling for gay organizations to be transgender-inclusive and were now attacking a human rights approach for not being exclusive enough. In retrospect, it is difficult to see how excluding gay, feminist, or straight Americans is ethically superior to excluding transgendered people... or anyone else.

The only group today using transgression in its

widest and most uncritical descriptive sense is queer youth, who consistently prefix anything genderqueer with 'trans' or 'tranz.' Many such radical youth are taking civil rights to the next level, finally making the long-delayed connection among gay, feminist, and trans politics.

It is still an open question if *genderqueer*, a word promoted to resolve some of these issues, will yet create its own hierarchies and exclusions

The New Gay

What began as the "gay community," then the "lesbian and gay community" (make sure not to erase women, put them first to make up for historic injustices), then the "lesbian, gay, and bisexual community" (append bisexuals whenever we remember to, don't forget they get oppressed too for sleeping with the same sex, wish they'd finally choosen one sex or the other and stop passing themselves off as straight—or gay—when it's convenient), has finally become—for all practical purposes (except when one was being quoted in *The New York Times* or *CNN*, you know, something important)— the "lesbian, gay, bisexual, and transgender community."

The term *LGBT* is still uncomfortable for some people. Some gays and lesbians can still be heard asking quietly, in their more politically incorrect moments, 'Why—I mean, I know, I shouldn't even think this, let alone say it—but why does changing your gender/sex belong in a movement about sexual orientation?' A good question if you think that sexual orientation and gender are separate. An even better question if you are fortunate enough to look, well... straight.

But there is no denying that after a persistent 10-year struggle, the *T* in *LGBT* is here to stay. Will the new gay embrace of transgender be successful? Will gay rights finally devote any real resources to transgender, and, if so, will they give us anything more than transsexual rights, and look further to those who are crossdressers, genderqueer, intersex, or nonbinary?

On this, the jury is still out. Although a few organizations have led the way, most organizations have not brought to bear anything like real muscle, and what muscle there is continues to be channeled into 'gender identity' and transsexual concerns.

In the meantime, the gay rights movements own "indigenous" genderqueers—stone butches, drag queens, fairies, high femmes and sissy boys --remain completely banished from civil discourse. They are never mentioned in public statements by any major progressive organization. For political purposes, they do not and never have existed.

Gender itself remains invisible as a progressive issue. If it is mentioned at all, it is carefully confined to transgender. In effect, *gender* has become the new *gay*. It is the thing we no longer speak about in polite company. I think here of school bullying, which is all about gender. People are paying attention to it now because, unfortunately, some victims shot their classmates. These are terrible crimes. But is the gender-bashing of school age youths new? Hasn't it been a regular feature of schools since there were classrooms and young boys in them? Or did we just overlook it because sissy boys are not a gay, feminist, or even a gender identity issue?

With gender stretched across the whole surface of

individuals' relations with society, maybe it's time to quit attacking the problem piecemeal, waiting for the next issue to appear on the front page of *The New York Times*. Maybe it's time to acknowledge a rigid gender system as a problem that impacts almost everyone, as a human rights issue for all.

About the Author

Riki Wilchins has been a leading advocate for gender rights and gender justice for 20 years, one of the founders of modern transgender political activism in the 1990s, and one of its first theorists and chroniclers. In 1995 Riki launched The Transexual [sic] Menace, the first national transgender street action group, which spread to 41 cities. The following year they launched GenderPAC, the first national political advocacy group devoted to gender identity rights. Riki was an early supporter in the launch of the intersex rights movement, as well as the movement for alternative sexualities.

They are the author of five books on gender theory and politics: *Read My Lips: Sexual Subversion & the End of Gender; Queer Theory/Gender Theory: An Instant Primer*; and *Voices from Beyond the Sexual Binary* (with editors Claire Howell and Joan Nestle), and this volume. Riki's writing and research on gender norms have been published in periodicals like the *Village Voice, GLQ, Research on Adolescence* and *Social Text, and* anthologies including *Contemporary Debates in the Sociology of Education, Gender Violence, Feminist Frontiers, Language Awareness, Negotiating Ethical Challenges in Youth Research, Out at Work, Women on Women* and *The Encyclopedia of Identity*. Riki has done trainings on gender norms and nonconformity at the White House, the Centers for Disease Control and the Office on Women's Health.

The New York Times has profiled Riki's work; in 2001 *Time Magazine* selected them as one of "100 Civic Innovators for the 21st Century." Riki is currently working on a book titled *Gender Transformative Practice: A Guide for Funders, Policy-makers, Practitioners, Parents—and the Rest of Us.*

Other Riverdale Avenue Books/Magnus Titles You Might Like By Riki Wilchins

TRANS/Gressive: How Transgender Activists Toon on Gay Rights, Feminism, the Media and Congress

Read My Lips: Sexual Subversion and the End of Gender

Queer Theory, Gender Theory: And Instant Primer

***

Hiding in Plain Sight
By Zane Thimmesch-Gill

Finding Masculinity: Female to Male Transition in Adulthood
Edited by Alexander Walker and Emmett J.P. Lundberg

Outside the XY: Queer, Black and Brown Masculinity
Edited by Brooklyn Boihood

*Queering Sexual Violence:
Radical Voices from Within the Anti-Violence Movement*
Edited by Jennifer Patterson